Editorial Project Manager
Lorin Klistoff, M.A.

Editor-in-Chief
Sharon Coan, M.S. Ed.

Illustrator
Kelly McMahon

Cover Artist
Brenda DiAntonis

Art Manager
Kevin Barnes

Art Director
CJae Froshay

Imaging
Rosa C. See

Product Manager
Phil Garcia

Publisher
Mary D. Smith, M.S. Ed.

Book 3

PHONICS

The gerbil plays guitar on the giraffe.

Authors

Kathy Dickinson Crane & Kathleen Law

Teacher Created Resources, Inc.
6421 Industry Way
Westminster, CA 92683
www.teachercreated.com

ISBN-0-7439-3017-7

©*2004 Teacher Created Resources, Inc.*

Reprinted, 2005

Made in U.S.A.

Table of Contents

Introduction

According to research, phonics is a key element of reading. Phonics refers to letter-sound relationships and to the rules that affect those relationships. Phonics instruction helps students connect sounds to letters, decode words, and recognize patterns in words.

Current research indicates that phonics instruction should be a part of a balanced reading program. Furthermore, it should be actively practiced and used well beyond the first year of reading.

This workbook, *Phonics: Book 3*, provides practice in phonics skills for readers who are becoming more proficient. *Phonics: Book 3* is part of a three-book series. As the third workbook in this companion series, it provides practice and review of all phonics introduced in the first two workbooks. A review of each phonics rule is also provided as the related skill is practiced.

This workbook has been designed as a tool for additional practice for students moving into greater proficiency and independence in reading. Consonants, vowels, blends, digraphs, and diphthongs are reviewed. Base words, suffixes, synonyms, and antonyms will be explored. Dictionary skills will be developed, helping students become even more independent.

Reading is a life-long skill that impacts every area of learning. Through research, we know that certain elements must be accounted for as children become readers. The activities in this workbook address and review important reading skills and provide an opportunity for independent practice of these reading skills. When used in conjunction with a phonics-based reading program, this workbook will strengthen the learner's ability to read.

UNIT 1

Consonants, Hard and Soft c and g

Initial Consonants

Directions: Listen for the sound at the beginning of each zoo animal. Write the letter for the beginning sound in the box by the animal.

Initial Consonants

Directions: Draw a picture for each initial consonant listed. Write the picture name on the line.

b _____	c _____	d _____	f _____
g _____	h _____	j _____	l _____
m _____	n _____	q _____	s _____
v _____	w _____	y _____	z _____

Initial Consonants

Directions: Read each sentence. Circle the word that completes the sentence and write it on the line.

1. Tom is going on a _____.

drip   trip   lip

2. He is going on a _____.

ship   sip   tip

3. It is almost time for him to _____.

sack   tack   pack

4. He will take just one big _____.

tag   bag   lag

5. Tom will be gone for seven _____.

days   ways   jays

6. His dad said he will get to _____.

dish   fish   wish

7. He also plans to swim and _____.

live   hive   dive

8. It sounds like he will have a lot of _____.

bun   fun   pun

Medial Consonants

Directions: Name the letter in the first box. Circle each picture in the row that has the sound of that letter in the middle of the word.

Medial Consonants

Directions: Listen for the sound in the middle of each item on the store shelf. Write the letter for the sound in the box by the grocery item.

Medial Consonants

Directions: Read each sentence. Circle the word that completes the sentence and write it on the line.

1. John plans to marry a nice _____.

   lady   lately

2. She lives in a very large _____.

   carry   city

3. I think that she is _____.

   penny   pretty

4. I get to be in the _____.

   wedding   wagon

5. I wish I could arrive on a _____.

   poppy   pony

6. Instead, we will ride in a _____.

   litter   limo

7. The bride will carry _____.

   daisies   daggers

8. At the end, we will let the _____ fly!

   balloons   baboons

Final Consonants

Directions: Write the final consonant sound for each picture.

1.	2.	3.	4.
_____	_____	_____	_____

5.	6.	7.	8.
_____	_____	_____	_____

9.	10.	11.	12.
_____	_____	_____	_____

13.	14.	15.	16.
_____	_____	_____	_____

Final Consonants

Directions: Rhyming words have the same ending sound. Write a rhyming word for each picture.

list	mist	bus	
whale		drum	
crown		chair	
sink		sheep	
bride		king	
knife		ship	
egg		block	
dove		bed	

Final Consonants

Directions: Read each sentence. Circle the word that completes the sentence, and write it on the line.

	1. Jill needed to get a _____ .	gill give gift
	2. She went to a toy _____ .	shop shot shod
	3. She saw a baseball _____ .	ban bad bat
	4. "I'll give this and a _____ ."	bag ball bat
	5. She added a _____ .	can cat cap
	6. Her _____ was too small.	box bog boss
	7. She put it all in a _____ .	bat ban bag
	8. It is for a friend who is _____ .	sit six sip

Consonant Review

Directions: Name each picture. Listen for the sound of the letter in the box. If you hear it at the beginning of the word, write the letter in the first space. If you hear it in the middle, write it in the second space. If you hear the sound at the end of the word, write the letter in the last space.

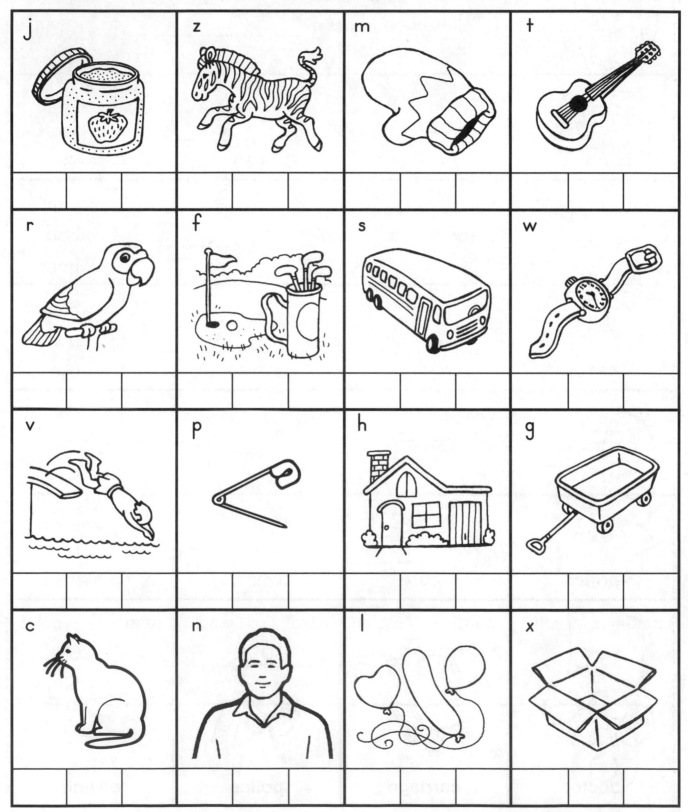

Hard and Soft c

Directions: Say the name of each picture. If the **c** sound is hard as in *cap*, circle the word **hard**. If the **c** sound is soft as in *mice*, circle the word **soft**.

hard soft	hard soft	hard soft	hard soft
city	**candy**	**coat**	**pencil**

hard soft	hard soft	hard soft	hard soft
castle	**celery**	**ice**	**coins**

hard soft	hard soft	hard soft	hard soft
prince	**cub**	**cymbals**	**cookies**

hard soft	hard soft	hard soft	hard soft
doctor	**carriage**	**police**	**ceiling**

Hard and Soft c

Directions: Read the rule below. Write the words that contain a hard sound in the cube. Write the words that contain a soft sound in the circle.

RULE

When the letter **c** is followed by the vowels **a**, **o**, or **u**, it has the hard sound. Hard **c** has the **k** sound found in the word *cube*. When **c** is followed by **e**, **i**, or **y**, it usually has a soft sound. Soft **c** has the **s** sound found in the word *city*.

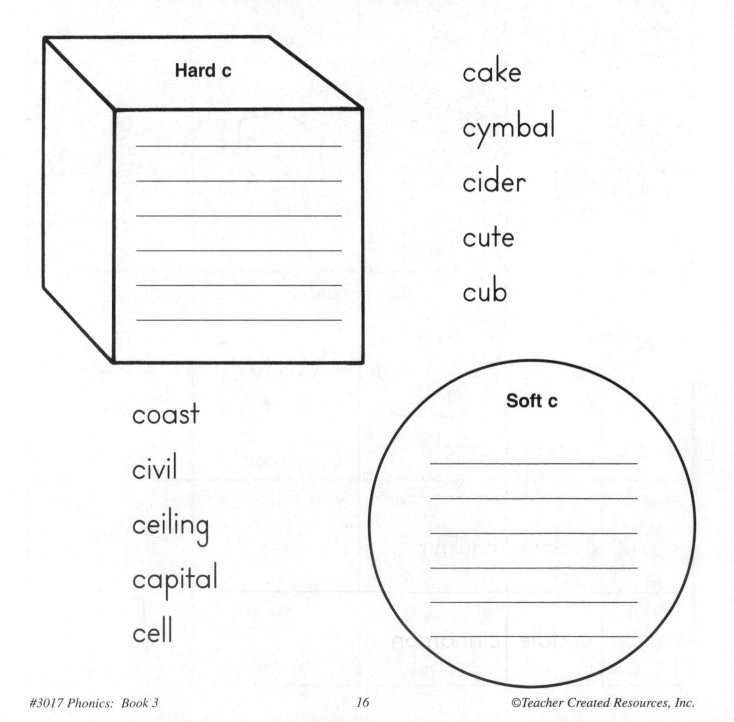

Hard c

cake

cymbal

cider

cute

cub

coast

civil

ceiling

capital

cell

Soft c

Hard and Soft c

Directions: Find a row with three pictures or three words with the **hard c** or the **soft c** sound. Draw a line through the three pictures or words. On the line, write if the matching sounds are **hard c** or **soft c** sounds.

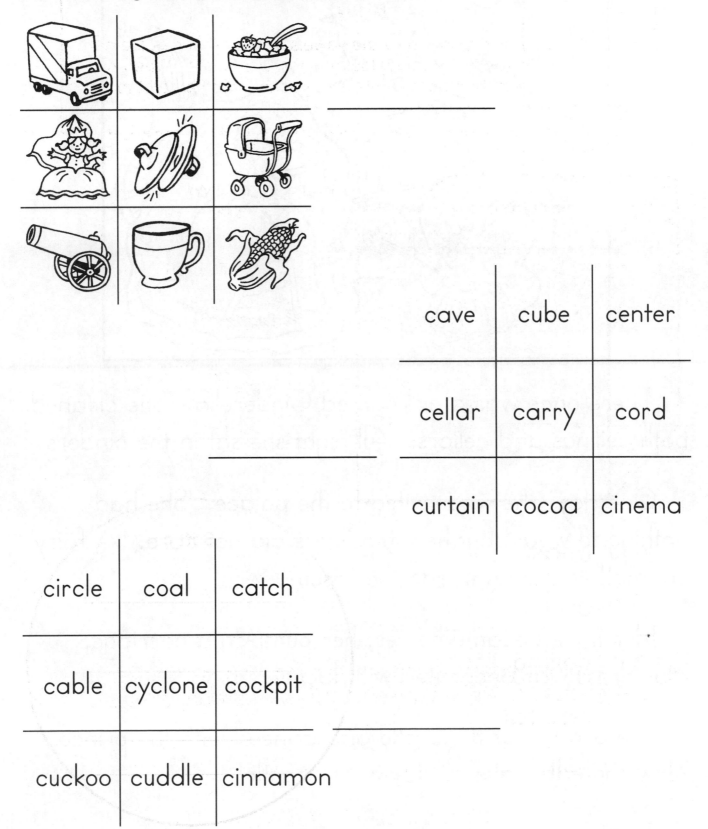

cave	cube	center
cellar	carry	cord
curtain	cocoa	cinema

circle	coal	catch
cable	cyclone	cockpit
cuckoo	cuddle	cinnamon

Hard and Soft c

Directions: Read the story below. Underline every word with a soft **c** sound. Circle every word with a hard **c** sound.

There once was a girl named Cinderella. She cleaned both ceilings and cellars. All night she sat in the cinders.

One day, she was invited to the palace. She had nothing to wear, but her stepsisters did not care. A fairy godmother soon came to the rescue.

Her mice became horses, her pumpkin a carriage. Her dress was decorated with lace.

She arrived at the castle and danced with the prince. Now she eats cake all day in her castle!

Hard and Soft g

Directions: Say the name of each picture. If the **g** sound is hard as in *go*, circle the word *hard*. If the **g** sound is soft as in *gym*, circle the word *soft*.

hard soft	hard soft	hard soft	hard soft
gondola	**giraffe**	**dragon**	**pledge**
hard soft	hard soft	hard soft	hard soft
giant	**judge**	**goose**	**gate**
hard soft	hard soft	hard soft	hard soft
carriage	**hug**	**golf ball**	**general**
hard soft	hard soft	hard soft	hard soft
game	**bridge**	**gem**	**guard**

Hard and Soft g

Directions: Read the rule below. Write the words that contain a hard sound, as in *gorilla*, under **Hard g**. Write the words that have a soft sound, as in *giraffe*, under **Soft g**.

RULE
When the letter **g** is followed by the vowels **a**, **o**, or **u**, it has the hard sound. When **g** is followed by **e**, **i**, or **y**, it usually has a soft sound.

giraffe   gorilla   gap   gypsy   gumdrop

genius   guppy   gentle   gallon   gondola

ginger   gym   guitar   gerbil

Hard g

_____

_____

_____

_____

_____

_____

_____

Soft g

_____

_____

_____

_____

_____

_____

_____

Hard and Soft g

Directions: Find a row with three pictures or words with the **hard g** or the **soft g** sound. Draw a line through the three pictures or words. On the line, write if the matching sounds are **hard g** or **soft g** sounds.

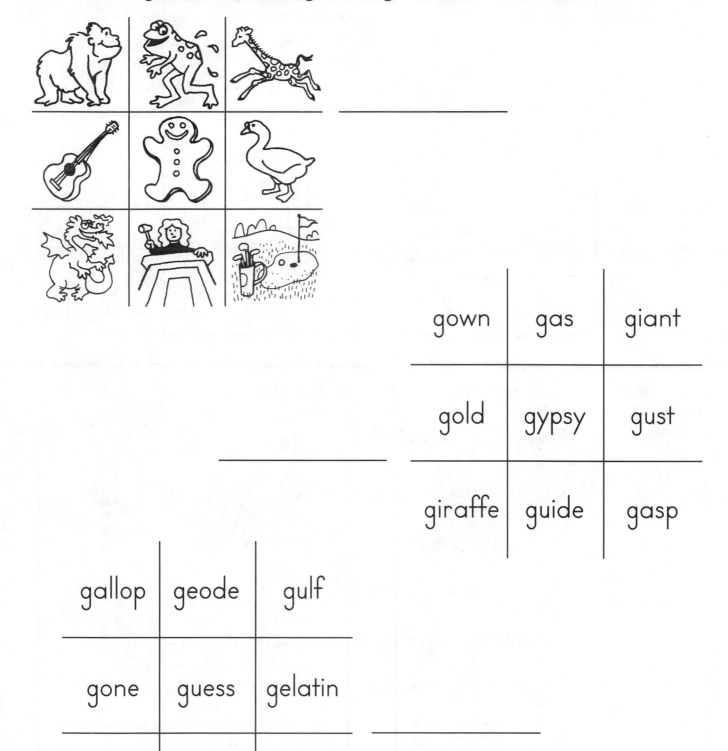

gown	gas	giant
gold	gypsy	gust
giraffe	guide	gasp

_____

gallop	geode	gulf
gone	guess	gelatin
geometry	germ	garden

_____

Hard and Soft g

Directions: Read the sentences below. Underline every word with a **soft g** sound. Circle every word with a **hard g** sound.

Across the bridge is a gate.

Inside the gate is a garden.

In the garden is a dragon.

It is guarding a tree for the giant.

The tree is growing huge oranges.

I think the oranges are magic!

I wish I had this grand garden.

My garden just has green grass!

Unit Review

Directions: Change beginning and final consonants to make new words. Can you change *mom* into *dad*?

Begin with *mom*.   **mom**

1. Change the final consonant to **p**. _____

2. Change the beginning consonant to **h**. _____

3. Change the beginning consonant to **t**. _____

4. Change the vowel **o** to **i**. _____

5. Change the beginning consonant to **n**. _____

6. Change the vowel **i** to **a**. _____

7. Change the beginning consonant to **r**. _____

8. Change the beginning consonant to **s**. _____

9. Change the final consonant to **d**. _____

10. Change the beginning consonant to **d**. _____

Unit Review

Directions: Use every word in the box to complete the chart below. Find three words that have the beginning, middle, and final consonant of that specific letter. Write the words in the correct columns.

comet	zipper	tick	balloon
quill	Missy	bus	butter
wagon	cave	wig	peacock
radio	summer	band	
ramp	lucky	heaven	
van	game	duck	

	Beginning Consonant	Middle Consonant	Final Consonant
s			
d			
l			
v			
g			
p			
t			

Unit Review

Directions: Read the words in the box. Circle them in the word find. All soft **c** or soft **g** words are across. All hard **c** or hard **g** words are down.

gang	comet	ago	cement	gym
city	cattle	gutter	recess	cyst
curly	giraffe	gone	gentleman	

x g y m c c y s t

t o y c u o l m g

p n s a r m i f a

g e n t l e m a n

u c i t y t n b g

t x i l w k p z a

t w c e m e n t g

e r e c e s s n o

r s g i r a f f e

Unit Review

Directions: Write the letter in the first, middle, or last space to match where the sound is heard in the word.

Directions: Use the words to solve the following riddles.

| yellow | queen | penguin | seven | candy |

1. a bird that swims _____

2. the color of bananas _____

3. something sweet to eat _____

4. she lives in a palace _____

5. the number after six _____

Unit Review

Directions: Read each word below. If it has a beginning hard **c** or hard **g** sound, circle the word.

goblet	cement	cackle	cycle
Cindy	gypsy	cents	giant
gander	gold	gym	city
cope	cupcake	candle	garden
gerbil	guess	gum	germ
cartoon			

Directions: Using the words in the box above, solve the following riddles.

1. a small pet _____

2. a pretty glass _____

3. it has a wick _____

4. a girl's name _____

5. it can make you sick _____

6. a funny show or drawing _____

UNIT 2

Short and Long Vowels

Short a

Directions: Say the name of each picture below. Color each picture that has the short **a** sound in its name.

Short i

Directions: Write the name of each picture below. Then circle the letter that represents the short **i** sound.

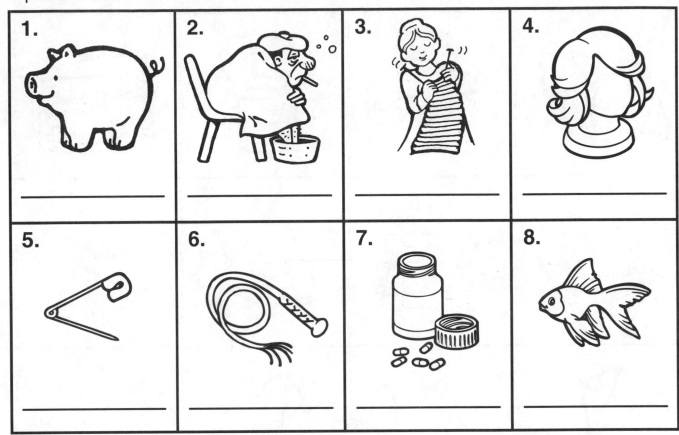

1.	2.	3.	4.
_____	_____	_____	_____

5.	6.	7.	8.
_____	_____	_____	_____

Directions: Read each word below. Print a word on the line that rhymes with each word that also has the short **i** sound.

9. jig _____

10. grip _____

11. lick _____

12. rip _____

13. lit _____

14. sick _____

15. ill _____

16. wig _____

17. twin _____

18. mitt _____

Short u

Directions: Write the name of each picture containing the short **u** sound. Then circle the vowel in each word.

1.	2.	3.	4.
____	____	____	____

5.	6.	7.	8.
____	____	____	____

Directions: Read the paragraph below. Circle the words that have the short **u** sound.

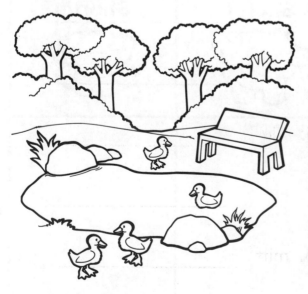

A Trip to the Duck Pond

One day Bud and his dad went to the duck pond. They got in their truck and drove down the bumpy road. When they arrived at the pond, Bud jumped out of the truck and ran off to have fun with the ducks. Dad took some gum out of his pocket and stood and watched as Bud was running after the ducks. They had a lot of fun at the pond. It was Bud's lucky day!

Short a, i, and u

Directions: Read each word in the first column. Change the short **u** to short **a**. Write the new word in the second column. Then change the short **a** to short **i** and write the new word in the third column.

Short u Word	Short a Word	Short i Word
lump		
jug		
bun		
yuck		
sunk		
sup		
hum		
rug		
rum		
but		

Directions: Sort the words below into the correct short vowel column.

had   bin
fit   sip
rip   plug
bun   ban
sash   cap
fun   grit
brat   sill
sub   will
pin   slug
flat   gash
rug   fit

Short a	Short i	Short u

Short o

Directions: Write the name of each picture containing the short **o** sound. Then find and circle each word in the search below.

1.

_____

c	m	o	p	d	c	o	o	b	g
i	q	l	o	o	o	d	d	j	o
o	p	i	t	o	d	c	f	g	r
e	o	v	k	n	o	c	k	f	i
p	m	e	d	c	c	l	o	r	c
p	o	s	o	c	k	o	b	o	o
o	n	l	u	i	e	c	d	g	t
n	d	o	r	o	c	k	m	c	k
d	o	g	h	o	u	s	e	o	d

2.

_____

3.

_____

4.

_____

5.

6.

7.

8.

_____   _____   _____   _____

9.

10.

11.

12.

_____   _____   _____   _____

Short e

Directions: Write the name of each picture below. Then circle the letter that represents the short **e** sound.

1.

2.

3.

4.

_____

5.

6.

7.

8.

_____

Directions: Circle the words with a short **e** in the list below. Then circle those words in the puzzle.

sled   vet

pest   den

cat   tell

rent   head

bell   bun

p	e	b	u	n
e	r	e	n	t
s	d	l	s	c
t	e	l	l	a
e	n	v	e	t
h	e	a	d	e

Short o and e

Directions: Write about a trip you have taken. Use some of the words below containing the short **o** and **e** vowel sounds.

box	bed	top	cop	cob
lock	on	tent	not	pen
sock	doll	went	men	sent

Short Vowels Review

Directions: Follow the instructions to make *jet* into a new word.

Begin with *jet*.   jet

1. Change the j to b.   _____

2. Change the e to u.   _____

3. Change the u to i.   _____

4. Change the i to a.   _____

5. Change the t to n.   _____

6. Change the a to u.   _____

7. Change the u to i.   _____

8. Change the b to f.   _____

9. Change the i to u.   _____

10. Change the u to a.   _____

11. Change the f to t.   _____

12. Change the a to i.   _____

13. Change the i to o.   _____

14. Change the t to w.   _____

15. Change the o to i.   _____

16. Change the n to t.   _____

17. Change the i to e.   _____

18. Change the w to j.   _____

Short Vowels Review

Directions: Match the scrambled letters below with one of the words in the box. Write the word on the line.

| hog |
| cross |
| strong |
| hug |
| sum |
| hung |
| frog |
| flag |
| flat |
| quit |
| went |
| guest |
| trip |
| test |

1. setug _____

2. rfog _____

3. gho _____

4. ttse _____

5. csors _____

6. lfga _____

7. tiqu _____

8. nosgtr _____

9. tpir _____

10. ugh _____

11. gnuh _____

12. msu _____

13. ntew _____

14. tfla _____

Directions: Write six sentences below using at least one of the scrambled words in each sentence.

_____

- -

_____

- -

_____

- -

_____

- -

_____

- -

_____

- -

_____

Long a

Directions: Fill in the bubble by the word that names each picture. Remember, if a one-syllable word has two vowels, the **first vowel** usually stands for the **long sound**, and the **second vowel** is **silent**. If the first vowel is **a**, the word has the **long a** sound.

1.
○ rack
○ rake
○ race

2.
○ cake
○ sake
○ sack

3.
○ grab
○ grate
○ grapes

4.
○ chant
○ chain
○ change

5.
○ plant
○ plat
○ plate

6.
○ snake
○ snack
○ sake

7.
○ male
○ mail
○ nail

8.
○ sale
○ sail
○ cell

9.
○ smell
○ sail
○ snail

10.
○ game
○ gram
○ came

11.
○ rain
○ reign
○ rane

12.
○ plank
○ plan
○ plane

Long i

Directions: Fill in the bubble by the word that names each picture. Remember, if a one-syllable word has two vowels, the **first vowel** usually stands for the **long sound**, and the **second vowel** is **silent**. If the first vowel is **i**, the word has the **long i** sound.

1. ○ dine ○ dice ○ diet	**2.** ○ bride ○ bid ○ bird	**3.** ○ pint ○ pine ○ pin
4. ○ lifeguard ○ lighthouse ○ chairlift	**5.** ○ snail ○ smell ○ smile	**6.** ○ slant ○ slid ○ slide
7. ○ lion ○ lone ○ line	**8.** ○ tight ○ tie ○ time	**9.** ○ icee ○ isn't ○ ice
10. ○ tint ○ tight ○ tiger	**11.** ○ knife ○ knot ○ nifty	**12.** ○ pie ○ pint ○ pry

Long u

Directions: Complete each sentence below by writing the word that names the long **u** picture. Remember, if a one-syllable word has two vowels, the **first vowel** usually stands for the **long sound**, and the **second vowel** is **silent**. If the first vowel is **u**, the word has the long **u** sound.

duet   flute   Utah   uniforms   tuba   June   tune

1. Next _____ the band will go on a trip.

2. They will travel to _____ .

3. The band will wear their new _____ .

4. Jewel will be playing the _____ .

5. Ruel will play the _____ .

6. The band will play a happy _____ .

7. Sue and Jude will sing a _____ .

Long a, i, and u

Directions: Read the words below the chart. Listen for the long vowel sound. Write the words in the correct column.

long u word	long a word	long i word

blue	bite	rain	bride	mice
tuba	brake	cake	flute	suit
whale	name	line	fruit	tune
pipe	shake	fine	Spain	wail
cute	shame	mile	tube	spine

Long o

Directions: Find and circle the long **o** words in the puzzle. Write a sentence for four of the words. Circle the word in each sentence with a long **o** vowel sound. Remember, if a one-syllable word has two vowels, the first vowel usually stands for the long sound, and the second vowel is silent. If the first vowel is **o**, the word has the long **o** sound.

e	o	g	e	o	g	n	m	m	d
c	l	o	s	e	y	i	p	o	l
o	o	a	o	v	r	h	x	p	t
a	o	t	l	d	m	o	l	e	h
t	r	r	d	r	o	p	e	m	r
o	r	c	j	o	k	e	x	f	o
s	o	l	d	a	o	e	n	o	a
q	d	m	i	d	r	s	d	l	t
w	e	s	p	o	k	e	p	d	b
i	s	b	c	w	r	o	t	e	o

goat
close
hope
joke
mole
mope
road
rode
rope
sold
coat
fold
spoke
throat
wrote

1. _____

2. _____

3. _____

4. _____

Long e

Directions: Read the story. In the story, circle all the words that contain the letter **e** and have a long **e** sound. Answer the questions below and write the correct answer on the line to finish each sentence. Remember, if a one-syllable word has two vowels, the first vowel usually stands for the long sound, and the second vowel is silent. If the first vowel is **e**, the word has the long **e** sound.

A Story About Pete

Pete lived in Detroit. He loved living in the city. He lived in a green house a few feet from the park. Inside the large park were many trees and a zoo.

Pete and his sister Jean loved to visit the zoo. They would watch the seals play in the water. They loved to see the eagles in their nests. But Jean loved the lion the best. She liked to look at his large teeth.

Pete's family loved living in the city. There was always fun to greet them each day.

1. Pete lived in _____ .

2. He lived in a _____ house.

3. There were many _____ in the park.

4. Pete's sister was named _____ .

5. The _____ played in the water.

6. The _____ were in a nest.

7. Jean loved to watch the _____ .

8. The lion had large _____ .

Long e and o

Directions: Read the words in the maze below. Follow the trail of long **e** and **o** words to attach the wheel to the wagon.

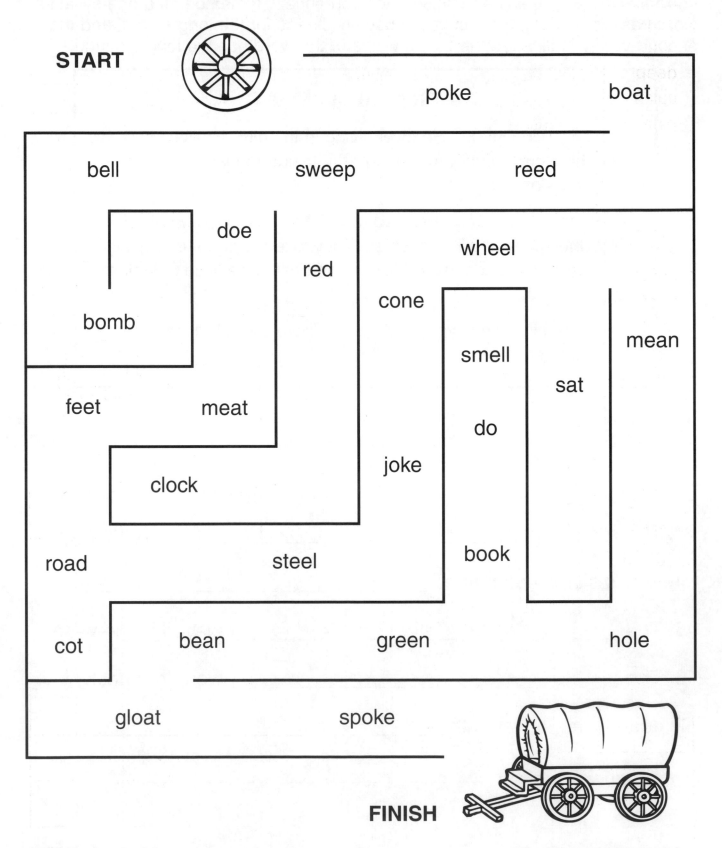

START

poke   boat

bell   sweep   reed

doe

bomb   red

wheel

cone

mean

smell

sat

feet   meat

do

clock   joke

book

road   steel

cot   bean   green   hole

gloat   spoke

FINISH

Long Vowels Review

Directions: Use the clues and the words in the box below to write the long vowel words in each puzzle.

Word Box
cone
nine
deep
cake
pine
eel
kite
lie
meat
June
cute
fleet
heat
nail
rain
leap

Across

1. The sun gives _____ .
3. The _____ is falling.
6. There was a _____ of ships.
8. The puppy is _____ .
10. Don't tell a _____ .
12. I like to eat _____ .
14. The tree is a _____ .
16. I want an ice cream _____ .

Down

2. The frog can _____ .
4. I want a birthday _____ .
5. A hammer and a _____
7. The water is _____ .
9. _____ is after May.
11. The _____ flies high.
13. After eight comes _____ .
15. The _____ lives in water.

Long Vowels Review

Directions: Use some of the long vowel words in the box below to write a letter to a friend describing your school.

rules	sweet	smile
notes	teacher	life
make	sleep	tune

_____

(Date)

Dear _____,

_____

_____

_____

_____

_____

_____

_____

_____

_____

_____

_____

Love,

_____

Short and Long Vowel Review

Directions: Write the name of each picture in the correct train car matching the long vowel sound.

Long **u**   Short **u**

Long **e**   Short **e**

Long **a**   Short **a**

Long **i**   Short **i**

Long **o**   Short **o**

 #3017 Phonics: Book 3

Short and Long Vowel Review

Directions: Read the words below and listen for the long and short vowel sounds. Write the words in the correct column.

lad	crate	rain	brain	wham	span
chat	heel	weep	sweet	wren	slice
pride	wife	twill	spin	spine	throat
fog	broke	drop	spot	hug	trump
bell	hand	team	gift	tune	top
suit	flute	came	cane	can	hose
hive	dock	game	rat	rate	jeep

Long a	Short a	Long i	Short i	Long o

Short o	Long e	Short e	Long u	Short u

48

Short and Long Vowel Review

Directions: Match the scrambled letters below with one of the words in the list. Write the word in each box.

lake
let
dug
dike
got
sad
keep
pig
goat
flute
flake
snake
sleet
mice
oat
tune
ton
tone
stop
quit

1. post	**2.** ceim	**3.** eetsl	**4.** eepk
5. klae	**6.** tiqu	**7.** gtoa	**8.** tlfeu
9. kflae	**10.** sakne	**11.** gip	**12.** etl
13. neot	**14.** ont	**15.** tog	**16.** gud
17. aot	**18.** dsa	**19.** uent	**20.** kied

Directions: Write five sentences below using at least one of the scrambled words in each sentence.

Unit Review

Directions: Circle the words in each box that have a **long vowel** sound. Underline the words with a **short vowel** sound.

1. stop   goat
    hope   hop
	2. bride bid
	    grin line
		3. game rain
		    bat can

4. feet   leap
    rent   get
	5. flute fuel
	    fun bud
		6. write sand
		    ban kite

Directions: Say the name of each picture below. Write its name on the line. Color the pictures whose names contain the long vowel sound.

7. _____

8. _____

9. _____

10. _____

11. _____

12. _____

Directions: Read each word. Change it to a word with a **long vowel** sound. Write the new word on the line.

13. tap _____	14. cop _____	15. ran _____
16. slid _____	17. can _____	18. tub _____

Unit Review

Directions: Say the name of each picture below. Fill in the circle beside the word with the same vowel sound.

1.	2.	3.	4.	5.
○ cake ○ bat ○ man	○ tone ○ pane ○ pie	○ ban ○ Gus ○ box	○ hot ○ hand ○ hat	○ rap ○ soap ○ drip
6.	**7.**	**8.**	**9.**	**10.**
○ bake ○ rag ○ slip	○ tuba ○ ton ○ tape	○ flat ○ fed ○ fast	○ pan ○ tin ○ hen	○ dish ○ dot ○ fan
11.	**12.**	**13.**	**14.**	**15.**
○ bat ○ gum ○ meat	○ sand ○ gum ○ came	○ bib ○ tub ○ kite	○ fix ○ tux ○ fox	○ stump ○ band ○ storm

Directions: Write nine short-vowel words, and write nine long-vowel words.

Words with a **short vowel** sound		

Words with a **long vowel** sound		

UNIT 3

Compounds, Blends, Digraphs, Y as a Consonant and as a Vowel, R-Controlled Vowels

Compound Words

Directions: Combine two words in each sentence to make a compound word to answer the riddle. Write the new word on the line.

> ## RULE
> A **compound word** is made up of two or more words joined together to make a new word. A *doghouse* is a *house* for a *dog*.

1. Corn that you pop is _____popcorn_____ .

2. A bird that is blue is a _____ .

3. A boat that will sail is a _____ .

4. A hive for a bee is a _____ .

5. A coat for the rain is a _____ .

6. A case for a book is a _____ .

7. A room for a bed is a _____ .

8. To dive in the sky is to _____ .

9. Light from a star is _____ .

10. A fish shaped like a star is a _____ .

11. A pot for tea is a _____ .

12. Seed for a bird is _____ .

13. A beam from the moon is a _____ .

14. A ball of meat is a _____ .

15. Bread made with ginger is _____ .

16. A gull from the sea is _____ .

17. A cake in a cup is a _____ .

18. A flower like the sun is a _____ .

Compound Words

Directions: Write the two words that make up the compound word. Then, find the compound word in the word search.

1. waterfall _____ _____

2. treetop _____ _____

3. Sunday _____ _____

4. postcard _____ _____

5. applesauce _____ _____

6. pancake _____ _____

7. seashell _____ _____

8. hairbrush _____ _____

9. cupcake _____ _____

10. necktie _____ _____

11. peanuts _____ _____

12. airway _____ _____

x	a	w	a	t	e	r	f	a	l	l
t	b	d	e	r	u	v	q	d	e	k
p	m	b	s	e	a	s	h	e	l	l
a	p	p	l	e	s	a	u	c	e	x
n	e	c	k	t	i	e	n	o	u	p
c	s	u	d	o	r	o	p	s	q	o
a	a	p	y	p	e	a	n	u	t	s
k	w	c	w	y	o	i	r	n	z	t
e	h	a	i	r	b	r	u	s	h	c
b	f	k	r	c	w	w	m	t	s	a
c	s	e	s	b	n	a	v	t	x	r
a	s	u	n	d	a	y	e	w	j	d

Syllables

Directions: Write the number of syllables that you hear in the box. Remember, words are made of syllables. You hear one vowel sound in each syllable.

Blends

Directions: Name the picture. Write its name on the line. Then circle the blend in each word.

A **consonant blend** is two or more consonants that come together in a word. Their sounds blend together, but each sound is heard.

R Blends Listen for the **r** blends as in *trap* and *drum*.	1.	2.	3.
4.	5.	6.	7.
L Blends Listen for the **l** blends as in *clock* and *glass*.	8.	9.	10.
11.	12.	13.	14.
S Blends Listen for the **s** blends as in *sled* and *stamp*.	15.	16.	17.
18.	19.	20.	21.

Blends

Directions: Read each word. Divide the words by blends. Write each word in the correct column.

stamp	swish	pretzel	clock	fruit	flute
spider	crowd	ski	glue	dream	blanket
glove	draw	scarf	flower	track	squirrel
princess	black	bride	sneak	grill	planet

r Blends	l Blends	s Blends

Blends

Directions: Complete each sentence with a word that contains a blend.

dream	trip	planets	brother	squirrels
class	spoke	slides	swings	playground
students	blocks	trains	trees	planetarium
bridge	planes	stars	studied	trucks

1. I have a _____ named Brett.

2. Brett has a great _____ at school!

3. Brett and his classmates can see the _____ from their room.

4. They can see other _____ when they are outside.

5. They like to watch them play on the _____ and _____ .

6. They also enjoy watching furry _____ climb up the _____ .

7. Once, Brett's class went on a field_____ .

8. The entire class walked eight _____ to the _____ .

9. Mrs. Franklin, the guide, _____ to the students.

10. She told them about the _____ and the _____ .

11. At another time, Brett's class _____ transportation.

12. They took a trip to a _____ that was close.

13. From there, they could see cars, _____ ,
_____ , and _____ .

14. I _____ of being in a class like Brett's!

Final Blends

Directions: Find the word that names the picture. Write it beside the picture. Underline the final blend.

camp	film	list	sand	tank	think
bunk	nest	bank	sling	rink	plant
sink	toast	vest	east		

1.

2.

3.

4.

5.

6.

7.

8.

9.

10.

11.

12.

13.

14.

15.

16.

Y as a Vowel

Directions: Say the name of each picture. Circle its name. If you hear the long **i** sound, write **i** on the line. If you hear the long **e** sound, write **e** on the line.

RULE

When **y** is the only vowel at the end of a one-syllable word, it usually has the long **i** sound as in *cry*. When **y** is the only vowel at the end of a word of more than one syllable, it usually has the long **e** sound as in *pony*.

1.
cry   dry

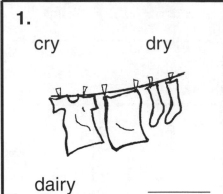

dairy   _____

2.
ferry   try

fry   _____

3.
fairy   dairy

fry   _____

4.
sly   sorry

sky   _____

5.
sorry   sunny

spy   _____

6.
marry   many

my   _____

7.
jelly   July

shy   _____

8.
sandy   cry

candy   _____

9.
shy   sty

sunny   _____

10.
candy   cherry

cry   _____

Y as a Consonant

Directions: Write the name of each picture. Remember, when **y** comes at the beginning of a word, it is a consonant.

yarn   yard   yolk   yak   yacht   yo-yo

1.	2.	3.
_____	_____	_____

4.	5.	6.
_____	_____	_____

Directions: Write the words with **y** in the correct column.

yellow	sly	pretty	young	try
fry	you	sty	many	yell
sorry	hurry	year	my	buddy

y as a consonant	y sound = long e	y sound = long i

Y as a Consonant and a Vowel

Directions: Complete the story with words that have the letter **y** in them. Write the words from the box on the lines.

butterfly	years	empty	cry	sky
Yesterday	Finally	by	spy	windy
pretty	happy	city	You	
try	yellow	puffy	My	
funny	fly	dry	shy	

_____ , my family took a walk in the _____ park.

1   2

The day was perfect! The _____ was full of _____ ,

3   4

white clouds. It wasn't _____ at all.

5

We walked for a long time. It felt like twenty _____! _____

6   7

dad found a bench so we could rest. It was _____ a water

8

fountain and had gotten a little wet. We hunted for a _____ bench.

9

We finally found one that was _____ .

10

_____ won't believe what happened next! A _____

11   12

flew right up to me! It seemed_____ about settling down. I

13

thought it would _____ away. _____, it landed on my

14   15

hand! The butterfly was so _____ . Its wings were black and

16

_____ .

17

I knew I had to _____ to be still, but then the butterfly walked on

18

my hand! It tickled and felt _____ . I started to laugh. I was so

19

_____ that I didn't even _____ when the butterfly

20   21

flew away. I hope I _____ another butterfly soon!

22

Consonant Digraphs

Directions: Write the name of each picture on the line. Circle the consonant digraph.

A **consonant digraph** consists of two consonants that together stand for one sound. Listen for the sound of **ch** in *chimp* and for the sound of **wh** in *whale*.

1. _____

2. _____

3. _____

4. _____

5. _____

6. _____

7. _____

8. _____

9. _____

10. _____

11. _____

12. _____

13. _____

14. _____

Digraphs

Directions: Read a word. Change the initial consonant with the digraph listed to make a rhyming word.

	Word	Digraph	Rhyme
1.	lurch	ch	church
2.	tip	sh	
3.	raw	gn	
4.	rink	th	
5.	list	wr	
6.	pale	wh	
7.	tot	kn	
8.	pool	sch	

Directions: Use the new words to complete the sentences.

9. I think she broke her _____ .

10. A _____ is a mammal, not a fish.

11. He rides the bus to _____ .

12. She tied a _____ in her shoelace.

13. You should _____ before answering the question.

14. Her cruise will be on that _____ .

15. That big building on the corner is a _____ .

16. Give the dog a bone to _____ .

Digraphs

Directions: Read the word. Write the digraph beside it. Fill in the bubble to show if the digraph is heard at the beginning, in the middle, or at the end of the word.

Word	Digraph	Position in Word		
1. teacher	ch	○	●	○
2. shout		○	○	○
3. brother		○	○	○
4. beach		○	○	○
5. beaches		○	○	○
6. sack		○	○	○
7. whale		○	○	○
8. knife		○	○	○
9. bathtub		○	○	○
10. shower		○	○	○
11. laugh		○	○	○
12. laughter		○	○	○
13. sign		○	○	○
14. whistle		○	○	○
15. write		○	○	○

R-Controlled Vowels

Directions: Say each picture name. Write it on the line, using some of the words in the list. Remember, an **r** after a vowel makes the vowel have a sound that is different from the usual long or short sound. Listen to the sound in *star* and *horn*.

flowers	yogurt	spider	burn	giraffe	nurse
letters	start	yard	germ	mother	ruler
hammer	parrot	yoga	sweater	weather	shore

1.

_____

2.

_____

3.

_____

4.

_____

5.

_____

6.

_____

7.

_____

8.

_____

9.

_____

10.

_____

11.

_____

12.

_____

R-Controlled Vowels

Directions: Read the riddle. Write the answer on the line.

morning	star	garden	circus	birthday	thirteen
thunder	bird	sister	sweater	turkey	yesterday
hurry	nurse	purple	horse	north	candy bar

1. your special day _____

2. opposite of south _____

3. place to grow vegetables _____

4. to go fast _____

5. day before today _____

6. early time of day _____

7. place with clowns and elephants _____

8. it goes with lightning _____

9. a sweet treat _____

10. mix red and blue for _____

11. a twinkle in the sky _____

12. takes care of sick people _____

13. you can ride this _____

14. number before fourteen _____

15. it keeps you warm _____

16. it gobbles _____

17. she's related to you _____

18. it chirps _____

R-Controlled Vowels

Directions: Complete each sentence with an r-controlled vowel word.

guitar	turned	Saturday	taller	surprised
summer	bigger	grandfather	porch	party
farmer	farm	fertilizer	barn	tractor
working	corn	favorite	hard	river

1. My _____ is a _____ .

2. He raises _____ and wheat.

3. I like to visit his _____ in the _____ .

4. Grandpa lets me ride on the _____ .

5. Some days we take_____ out to the fields.

6. It helps the corn grow _____ .

7. When the corn is completely grown, it will be _____ than my grandpa!

8. Everyone works _____ on the farm, but we also have fun.

9. Sometimes we sit on the _____ and my grandpa plays his _____ .

10. Once we had a _____ and danced in the _____ .

11. One summer my grandpa _____ me.

12. We took a _____ drive to the _____ .

13. Instead of _____ , we had a picnic. We also went swimming and fishing.

14. That day _____ out to be my _____ day of the summer!

Syllables

Directions: Circle the three pictures in each row that have the same number of syllables. How many syllables do you hear in the matching pictures? Write the answer in the small box. Remember, the letters *ar, or, ir, ur,* and *er* each have one vowel sound.

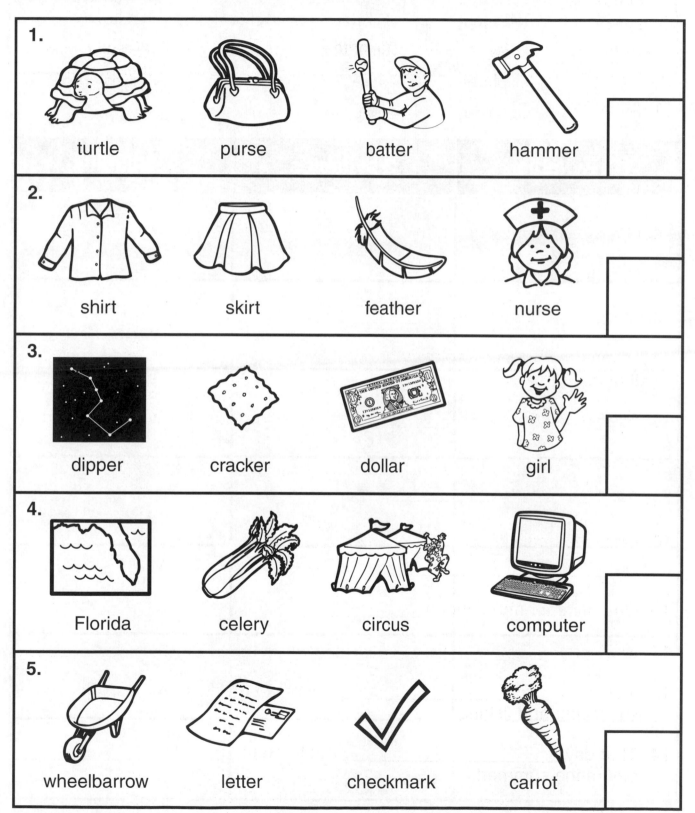

1.

turtle   purse   batter   hammer

2.

shirt   skirt   feather   nurse

3.

dipper   cracker   dollar   girl

4.

Florida   celery   circus   computer

5.

wheelbarrow   letter   checkmark   carrot

Syllables

Directions: Read each word. Count the number of syllables in it. Write the word in the correct list.

fry	dragon	clock	milkweed	computer
wheat	telephone	ticket	chocolate	shower
yam	know	umbrella	cry	countertop
dustpan	elephant	yipee	candy	yesterday
wrote	Saturday	wish	silly	

1 syllable	2 syllables	3 syllables

Syllables

Directions: Words often have vowels that you do not hear. Look at each word. In the first column, write the number of vowels that you see. In the second column, write the number of vowels that you hear. In the third column, write the number of syllables that you hear.

		see vowels	hear vowels	hear syllables			see vowels	hear vowels	hear syllables
1.	sweater				2.	peach			
3.	wheelbarrow				4.	thermometer			
5.	shutter				6.	knee			
7.	train				8.	whistle			
9.	school				10.	pliers			
11.	teacher				12.	spider			
13.	clarinet				14.	baby			
15.	flame				16.	umbrella			

Unit Review

Directions: Read each clue at the bottom of the page. Find the answer using the word list at the top of the page and write it in the crossword puzzle.

turtle	under	crow	yes	chips	star
short	dirty	stamp	shy	throne	plum

Down

1. a black bird

2. bashful

3. animal with a shell

5. not clean

7. fruit

8. twinkles in the sky

Across

1. something to eat

2. not tall

4. opposite of over

6. goes on a letter

9. a king sits on this

10. opposite of no

Unit Review

Directions: Write each word in the correct box.

drink	why	frame	turkey	shop	know
curtain	smoke	purse	thick	her	stamp
chimney	girl	car	plane	tough	south
gruff	better	wrap	blue	for	clap

Blends	Digraphs	R-Controlled Vowels

Unit Review

Directions: Count the syllables in the compound word. Write that number in the box. Then, write the two words that make up the compound word on the lines.

1. waterfall ☐ _____ _____

2. railroad ☐ _____ _____

3. classmate ☐ _____ _____

4. butterfly ☐ _____ _____

Directions: Underline the r-controlled vowel in each word. Then write the number of syllables on the line.

5. sport _____ 6. thunder _____ 7. star _____

8. dark _____ 9. purple _____ 10. chirp _____

11. circus _____ 12. flower _____ 13. tiger _____

14. slurp _____ 15. horn _____ 16. church _____

Directions: Write the word's blend on the line.		**Directions:** Write the word's digraph on the line.	
17. lamp _____	18. flag _____	25. knife _____	26. wrote _____
19. clown _____	20. bride _____	27. shop _____	28. beach _____
21. grass _____	22. play _____	29. white _____	30. mother _____
23. most _____	24. train _____	31. sack _____	32. sign _____

Directions: Read the words. Write each word in the correct box.

Ty   sandy   shy   yo-yo   happy   yolk

Y as a Consonant	Y = Long e sound	Y = Long i sound

Unit Review

Directions: Use the words to complete the story.

year	chocolate	July	friends	What
gift	finishing	yellow	beach	surprise
third	decorated	school	pretty	treehouse
whisper	backyard	secret	smiled	telephone
party	birthday	think	try	skywriter

Stacy, my sister, has her birthday on _____ _____ .
___1___ ___2___
Last year we had her party in our _____ . Dad built a
___3___
_____ and Mom _____ it with tiny _____
___4___ ___5___ ___6___
stars. Stacy _____ all day long. She couldn't wish for a nicer
___7___
_____ or a better birthday!
___8___

This _____ , we are planning a _____ party.
___9___ ___10___
We will celebrate Stacy's _____ this weekend at the
___11___
_____ . Twenty _____ from _____
___12___ ___13___ ___14___
will be at the _____ . Everyone will _____
___15___ ___16___
to keep the _____ .
___17___

Mom is baking a _____ cake. Dad is hiring a
___18___
_____ to spell "Happy Birthday" in the sky. Stacy's girlfriends
___19___
are calling on the _____ to _____
___20___ ___21___
about the party. I am _____ my present, a
___22___
_____ dress for Stacy to wear.
___23___

I _____ Stacy will smile again. _____
___24___ ___25___
do you think?

Unit 4

Contractions, Plurals, and Suffixes

Contractions

Directions: A **contraction** is a short way of writing two words. It is formed by putting two words together and leaving out one or more letters. An apostrophe (') is used to show where something is left out. An example would be "I will" changed to "I'll."

Read each sentence below and circle the contraction in each sentence. Then write the two words that make each contraction.

	Two Words	
1. (There's) a lot to do in New York.	There	is
2. He hasn't found his paper.		
3. There's a great movie in town!		
4. I've been learning to play the piano.		
5. What's the name of your pet?		
6. He's the best doctor in town.		
7. We've been to the dinosaur museum.		
8. He hasn't seen the ocean before.		
9. She doesn't miss school very often.		
10. We've been shopping all day.		
11. They're going to the concert.		
12. I couldn't go to the store.		
13. Isn't that a cute dress?		
14. I have a dog and you've a cat.		
15. We'll get out of school early today.		
16. There's a gray dog outside.		

Contractions

Directions: Read the story and circle each **contraction**. At the bottom of the page, write the two words that mean the same as each contraction you circled.

A Trip to the Movies

"Today is the day," said Mary. "I cannot wait to go to the movies with my family."

Mary and her family had planned a trip to the movies for Saturday. Mary and her brother Andy had been waiting all week to go.

"I'll buy some popcorn," said Andy.

"Okay," said Mary. "If you'll buy the popcorn, then I'll buy the candy and we'll share!"

Just then Mary and Andy heard their dad call to them.

"Come on kids," he said. "It's time to get moving! Let's go! We're going to be late if we don't hurry along."

Dad, Mom, Mary, and Andy all got into the car.

"We're off!" Dad said. "It shouldn't be long until we're in our seats ready for the movie to begin."

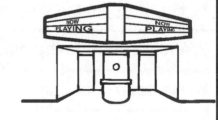

"I hope we aren't late," said Mary.

Soon the family was in their seats ready to watch a good movie and to have some great family fun.

"We shouldn't wait so long before out next movie trip," said Andy.

"Great," said Dad, "Let's plan another one."

"How about tomorrow?" said Mary. "Wouldn't that be fun?"

Plurals –s and –es

RULE

When **s** or **es** is added to a word, it forms the plural. "Plural" means more than one. See how the ending **s** or **es** makes these words mean more than one thing.

one apple → two apples   one box → two boxes

Directions: Circle the word that names each picture below. Color the pictures that show a plural.

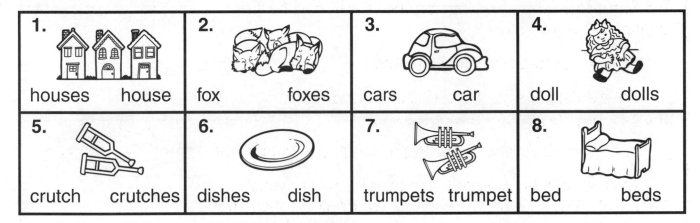

1. houses   house
2. fox   foxes
3. cars   car
4. doll   dolls
5. crutch   crutches
6. dishes   dish
7. trumpets   trumpet
8. bed   beds

RULE

If a word ends in **ss**, **x**, **ch**, or **sh**, add the ending **–es** to make it mean more than one.

one patch → two patches
one dress → two dresses
one brush → two brushes

Directions: Change each word into the plural form by adding the correct ending.

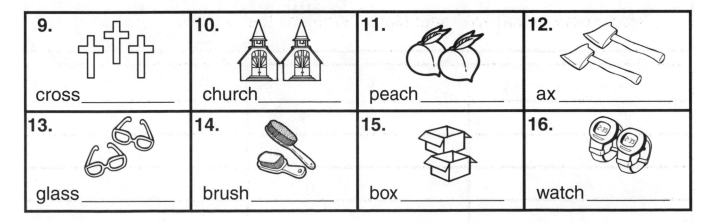

9. cross_____
10. church_____
11. peach_____
12. ax _____
13. glass_____
14. brush_____
15. box _____
16. watch_____

Plurals –s and –es

Directions: Write the plural form of each word on the line.

1. fly _____

2. enemy _____

3. baby _____

4. turkey _____

5. city _____

6. donkey _____

7. toy _____

8. lady _____

9. ray _____

10. worry _____

Directions: The word to which an ending is added is called the **base word**. Write the base word on the line beside its plural form.

11. patches _____

12. skies _____

13. boys _____

14. puppies _____

15. charities _____

16. armies _____

17. stories _____

18. monkeys _____

19. days _____

20. joys _____

Plurals –s and –es

Directions: Write the plural form of each word on the line.

1. knife

_____

2. wolf

_____

3. hoof

_____

4. leaf

_____

5. scarf

_____

6. calf

_____

7. half

_____

8. loaf

_____

Directions: Use a word from the box to complete each sentence. Remember to make it plural before you use it.

| calf | loaf | shelf | half | knife |

9. My dad keeps the sharp _____ in a safe place.

10. I think baby _____ are cute.

11. I have seven _____ of books in my room.

12. There are two _____ in one whole.

13. My mom baked two _____ of bread.

Endings –s, –es, –ed, and –ing

Directions: Read each word in the first column. Make new words by adding the endings **–s** or **–es**, **–ed**, and **–ing**. Write the new words in the correct

Base Word	Add s or es	Add ed	Add ing
1. dress			
2. jump			
3. look			
4. wash			
5. walk			

Directions: Write the base word for each of the following words.

6. snacks _____

7. caps _____

8. patches _____

9. foxes _____

10. heated _____

11. parking _____

12. starring _____

13. houses _____

14. loaded _____

15. crossing _____

Directions: Write three sentences of your own using at least three of the words above.

_____

_____

_____

_____

_____

Suffixes –er and –est

RULE

The suffix **er** may be used to compare two things. The suffix **est** may be used to compare more than two things.

Directions: Read each sentence. Add **er** or **est** to each word below the line. Write the new word on the line to complete the sentence.

1. Jack is _____ than his brother.
   smart

2. Sam is the _____ boy in his class.
   small

3. Of the whole class, Harry is the _____ storyteller.
   funny

4. My birthday party was my _____ day.
   happy

5. I hope that tomorrow will be the _____ day.
   great

6. The movie was the _____ of all.
   scary

7. I will be the _____ after the race.
   thirsty

8. Tammy is the _____ girl in the class.
   smart

RULE

The suffix **er** sometimes means "a person who." A preacher is a person who preaches.

Directions: Add the suffix **er** to each word and write the new word on the line.

9. preach _____   10. dance _____

11. talk _____   12. skate _____

13. play _____   14. write _____

15. walk _____   16. speak _____

17. read _____   18. watch _____

Plurals Review

Directions: Change some of the words into the plural form and use them as you write a story below. Make a tally mark for each plural word you are able to use. Write the total below.

boy

lady

worry

play

toy

bully

joy

buy

day

knife

wolf

sandwich

bath

bush

push

laugh

buzz

miss

bus

talk

Tally of plural words:

Total: _____

84 ©Teacher Created Resources, Inc.

Suffixes: Doubling Final Consonants

RULE
When a word with a short vowel ends in a single consonant, the consonant is usually doubled before adding a suffix that begins with a vowel.

Directions: Complete each sentence below by adding a suffix to the words in the box.

shop
swim
plan
win
hug
run
hit
dig

1. Jan was _____ out the door.

2. She _____ her dad before she left.

3. Soon she would be _____ in the sand.

4. Sam was _____ to play baseball.

5. His ball team had been _____ every game.

6. He had been _____ a home run each game.

7. Mother was going _____ at the mall.

8. David was happy he was going _____ in the pool.

Base Words

Directions: Write the base word for each of the following words.

9. sitting _____

10. begging _____

11. patting _____

12. hopped _____

13. sadder _____

14. stabbing _____

15. digger _____

16. slimmer _____

17. planned _____

18. tapping _____

Suffixes: Words Ending in Silent e

RULE

When a word ends in a silent **e**, drop the **e** before adding a suffix that begins with a vowel, such as **er**, **ed**, **ing**, or **est**.

Directions: Write a story below using at least five of the silent **e** words with the suffix. Circle those words in the story.

share + ing	skate + er	crave + ing
take + ing	race + ing	large + est
cute + er	make + ing	drive + er
bake + ed	name + ed	smile + ing

Suffixes Review

Directions: Read each sentence below. Complete the sentence by adding suffix to the word below the line. Write the new word.

1. Jill is _____ on crutches because of her broken leg.
   walk

2. She is _____ her leg will be better soon.
   hope

3. She has been _____ many stories from her favorite books.
   read

4. One story was about two baby wolves _____ in the forest.
   live

5. Jill loves _____ stories about animals.
   read

6. Her mother told her that reading a lot can make you _____ .
   smart

7. Jill's sister Sue was a ballet _____ .
   dance

8. She was very good at _____ .
   dance

9. Jill loved _____ the best.
   sing

10. She also thought that _____ was a lot of fun.
    swim

11. Jill's mom was _____ cookies in the kitchen.
    make

12. She soon was _____ the delicious taste of cookies.
    crave

13. Jill was soon _____ into the kitchen.
    head

14. She will be _____ once she tastes the warm cookies.
    happy

15. But she will be the _____ when her broken leg mends.
    happy

Suffixes Review

Directions: Make new words by adding suffixes to each base word. Write the new words in the correct columns.

Base Word	ing	ed
1. hug		
2. dance		
3. hop		
4. drag		
5. stun		
6. box		

Directions: Circle the word or words with a suffix in each sentence. Write the base word on the line.

7. John loved to drive everywhere. _____

8. He went to New York to do his Christmas shopping. _____

9. He is going to buy two scarves for his wife. _____

10. He will be giving them as gifts to her when he returns. _____

11. He is the happiest when he makes his wife happy. _____

12. John's wife is named Betty. _____

13. Betty is a teacher. _____

14. She likes teaching her class how to read. _____

Suffixes –ful, –less, –ly, and –ness

Directions: A **suffix** is a word part that is added at the end of a base word to change the base word's meaning or the way it is used. Add the suffix to each base word. Write the new word on the line.

1. alert + ness = _____

2. care + ful = _____

3. sick + ly = _____

4. taste + less = _____

5. dark + ness = _____

6. help + ful = _____

7. meek + ly = _____

8. weak + ness = _____

9. watch + ful = _____

10. low + ly = _____

Directions: Find the words in the puzzle below.

wonderful	homeless	saintly	gladly
hopeful	quickness	quickly	
illness	sadly	quietly	

h	g	l	a	d	l	y	h	l	q
o	d	n	e	s	c	w	o	c	d
m	e	q	n	l	s	o	p	s	k
e	q	u	i	c	k	n	e	s	s
l	u	i	l	o	l	d	f	a	a
e	i	e	l	d	n	e	u	y	i
s	c	t	n	d	r	r	l	o	n
s	k	l	e	a	x	f	d	x	t
l	l	y	s	e	n	u	t	i	l
h	y	s	s	a	d	l	y	l	y

Suffixes -er, -est, -ly, and -ness

Directions: Sort the words below into the window that matches its suffix.

carefully	sicker	neatest	louder	quickness
brightly	careless	greatest	helper	thankless
kindly	smaller	smallest	taller	hopeless
sadness	painless	neatness	sickly	calmness
madness	gladly	cuter	smartest	aimless

–ness

–less

–ly

–er

–est

Suffix –y

Directions: Add the suffix **–y** to each word. Write the new words on the lines. Then, circle the word that correctly completes the sentence below and write it on the line.

1. wind + y = _____

2. crunch + y = _____

3. snow + y = _____

4. rain + y = _____

5. itch + y = _____

6. sleep + y = _____

7. scare + y = _____

8. mess + y = _____

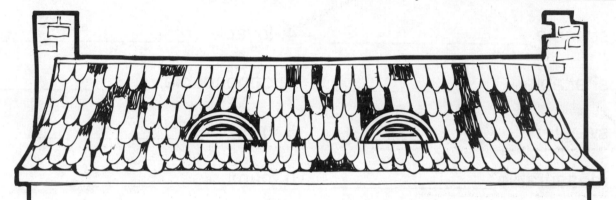

9. The haunted house was very _____ .

   happy   spooky

10. The broken steps were _____ and steep.

    speedy   squeaky

11. The steel rails were all very _____ .

    thirsty   rusty

12. A _____ sound whistled through the windows.

    dusty   windy

13. Outside the _____ weather continued.

    sleepy   rainy

14. Was I safer inside the _____ house or out in the rain?

    scary   snowy

15. I hear a _____ sound. Where is my umbrella?

    freaky   fluffy

Suffixes –en and –able

Directions: Read each word below and write its base word on the line beside it. Then find the words in the puzzle below.

1. tighten _____

2. loosen _____

3. suitable _____

4. lovable _____

5. shakable _____

6. dependable _____

7. sweeten _____

8. movable _____

9. measurable _____

10. namable _____

m	a	n	n	a	m	a	b	l	e	e	c	s	w	x
c	d	b	g	j	o	o	l	e	d	c	s	a	b	s
z	x	d	e	d	e	g	i	o	p	s	n	u	i	w
w	s	q	w	w	e	r	u	y	u	h	p	o	d	e
a	u	r	c	m	e	a	s	u	r	a	b	l	e	e
s	i	m	a	n	a	b	c	l	s	k	e	e	p	t
d	t	n	b	e	e	e	a	d	e	a	v	b	e	e
f	a	x	c	r	d	s	x	v	d	b	s	d	n	n
v	b	l	o	v	a	b	l	e	l	l	i	r	d	t
b	l	o	o	s	e	n	e	y	e	e	h	n	a	e
n	e	e	s	j	i	b	c	u	j	x	b	m	b	s
j	s	d	x	k	p	l	e	k	l	e	b	t	l	r
k	c	d	s	o	m	x	m	o	v	a	b	l	e	a
o	s	c	d	s	n	a	x	a	w	c	n	l	x	t
m	t	i	g	h	t	e	n	c	v	e	a	b	l	e

Suffixes –y, -en, and –able

Directions: Circle each word that has the suffix shown in the picture. Then write the base word on the line.

1. It was going to be a cold and snowy day. _____

2. It will be fun to play in the snow in the stormy weather. _____

3. The kids built a snowman from the frosty snow. _____

4. He was wearing a fluffy scarf. _____

5. He had a pointy carrot nose! _____

6. It will soon be time to brighten our home with a Christmas tree. _____

7. When we darken the room the lights will glow. _____

8. I will straighten the ornaments into a design. _____

9. Our tree will lighten the room. _____

10. It will soften all hearts to see the beautiful tree. _____

11. I will be giving a suitable gift to my brother. _____

12. I will give my dad something very likeable. _____

13. My mom wants a lovable puppy this year. _____

14. I will give my grandma something readable. _____

15. But I won't give the baby anything breakable! _____

Syllables in Words with Suffixes

Directions: A suffix that has a vowel sound forms a syllable by itself. Divide each word into syllables using a slash mark. Then write the syllables on the lines.

1. walking _____	2. growing _____
3. brighten _____	4. wishful _____
5. cupful _____	6. sledding _____
7. sweetly _____	8. crutches _____
9. wanted _____	10. writing _____
11. helpful _____	12. painter _____
13. cheery _____	14. rainy _____
15. sleepy _____	16. darkness _____
17. spinning _____	18. quickly _____
19. tallest _____	20. helpless _____
21. smaller _____	22. windy _____
23. running _____	24. lighten _____
25. sleeping _____	26. whiten _____
27. harmless _____	28. branches _____
29. skies _____	30. blows _____

Syllables in Words with Suffixes

Directions: Each word is divided into syllables. Put the syllables together to make the complete word.

1. neat + ness = _____

2. break + able = _____

3. cup + ful = _____

4. spoon + ful = _____

5. sad + ly = _____

6. teach + er = _____

7. luck + y = _____

8. light + en = _____

9. dark + ness = _____

10. hope + less = _____

11. paint + ing = _____

12. wait + ing = _____

13. help + er = _____

14. earn + est = _____

15. small + er = _____

16. work + er = _____

17. bright + ness = _____

18. use + less = _____

19. cheer + ful = _____

20. snow + y = _____

Directions: Write three sentences of your own using some of the words above. Circle the words you used from those.

_____

- -

_____

- -

_____

- -

Plurals and Suffixes Review

Directions: Say and spell each word. Write the words in the boxes where they belong.

crutches	bumped	boxes	loves	misses
watches	happier	worried	pens	sheets
dancing	seemed	jogging	makes	reading
worries	games	writing	tanning	scary
wonderful	brighten	snowy	helpless	brightness
stoppable	careful	whiten	pliable	darken
meekly	happiness	harmless	gladly	wiper

–s, –es	–ing, –er, –est, –ed

–ly, –ful, –less, –ness	–y, –en, –able

Plurals and Suffixes Review

Directions: Write about a day at the circus using several of the words in the list below.

bravest	scary	animals	clowns
circuses	roars	elephants	tigers
careful	watching	trainer	largest
played	helpless	jumping	played
slowly	darkness	teachable	useful
rainy	tricky	laughable	happiness

Unit Review

Directions: Circle the word that will finish each sentence then write it on the line.

1. Our class is going to _____ a program.	performed perform
2. We hope our _____ will be able to come.	parent parents
3. We have been _____ very hard.	practicing practiced
4. I love _____ the songs.	sing singing
5. Sue has been very _____ to the teacher.	helped helpful
6. She likes to help with the _____ .	decorations decorate
7. We have been making _____ .	snowflake snowflakes
8. Also, we have _____ made paper chains.	careful carefully
9. The boys have made cars out of _____ .	box boxes
10. Sam made the _____ car of all.	bigger biggest
11. _____ excited for tomorrow to put on the program.	We're Were
12. Today it is _____ not to be excited.	useless unless
13. _____ been practicing my part.	I've hive
14. _____ is falling. We are almost ready.	Darker Darkness
15. _____ the day! Welcome to our program.	Today Today's

Unit Review

Directions: Read the two words. Fill in the circle beside the correct contraction.

1. you + will	○ you'll ○ you're	2. they + are	○ they're ○ there	3. I + am	○ I'll ○ I'm
4. could + not	○ wouldn't ○ couldn't	5. it + is	○ it's ○ its	6. he + is	○ he's ○ his

Directions: Read the words and endings. Fill in the circle next to the correct spelling.

7. story + s	○ stories ○ storys	8. boy + s	○ boyes ○ boys
9. wolf + s	○ wolfs ○ wolves	10. mad + ly	○ maddly ○ madly
11. quiet + ness	○ quietness ○ quiteness	12. tall + est	○ tallest ○ talest
13. jump + ed	○ jumped ○ jumpped	14. hide + ing	○ hiding ○ hideing
15. tip + ing	○ tiping ○ tipping	16. use + less	○ useless ○ usless
17. cute + er	○ cuteer ○ cuter	18. lump + y	○ lumpey ○ lumpy

Directions: Write three complete sentences using at least one word with a suffix and a contraction in each sentence.

UNIT 5
Vowel Pairs, Digraphs, and Diphthongs

Vowel Pairs

RULE

In a **vowel pair**, two vowels come together to make one long vowel sound. When one syllable has a vowel pair, the first vowel stands for the long sound and the second vowel is silent. Vowel pairs include **ai**, **ay**, **ea**, **ee**, **ow**, **oa**, **oe**, and **ie**.

Directions: Write each word under the correct picture. Then circle the vowel pair in each word.

sailboat	goat	chain	teacher	tie	rowboat
teeth	pie	toes	tray	read	bowl

1.	2.	3.	4.
_____	_____	_____	_____

5.	6.	7.	8.
_____	_____	_____	_____

9.	10.	11.	12.
_____	_____	_____	_____

Vowel Pairs

Directions: Choose the word that will complete the sentence. Write it on the line.

1. This dog is a _____ .	spray stray
2. Have you ever heard a pig _____ ?	squeal steal
3. A female deer is a _____ .	doe do
4. After the storm, I saw a beautiful _____ .	raincoat rainbow
5. The kids went to the park to _____ .	pay play
6. When she saw the mouse, she _____ .	screamed streamed
7. If I had a castle, I would dig a _____ around it.	coat moat
8. How can I get this _____ out?	strain stain
9. I will hang a _____ on the door.	wreath weep
10. I bought my dad a _____ for Father's Day.	tea tie
11. We're going to see if our boats will _____ .	float gloat
12. Listen to the wind _____ .	blow glow
13. I need to check my e-_____ .	wail mail
14. I bought a new pair of _____ .	jeeps jeans

Vowel Pairs

Directions: Read the clue and the rhyming word. Then, drop the first consonant of the rhyme and replace it with one of the letters at the top of the page to solve the riddle. Write the answer in the third column.

| b | c | c | d | j | l | p | s | t | t |

Clue	Rhyme	Answer
vehicle used in the army	beep	1. _____
part of your foot	foe	2. _____
opposite of fast	glow	3. _____
24-hour period	ray	4. _____
piece of fruit	reach	5. _____
keeps you warm	goat	6. _____
opposite of dirty	glean	7. _____
a dog might wag it	pail	8. _____
to not tell the truth	pie	9. _____
you think with it	drain	10. _____

Vowel Pairs

Directions: Find two words with vowel pairs in each sentence. Write them in the boxes beside the sentence.

1. Kay took a trip on the train.		
2. She met Joe at the beach.		
3. I need to weed the garden.		
4. Fay just bought a new garden hoe.		
5. Do you like rain or snow the best?		
6. The water began to flow across the road.		
7. That tree is green all the time.		
8. I think I can eat the whole pie!		
9. What is your main fear?		
10. Did your plant grow or did it die?		

Vowel Pairs

Directions: Look at each word. In the first column, write the number of vowels that you see. In the second column, write the number of vowels that you hear. In the third column, write the number of syllables that you hear.

	number of vowels seen	vowels heard	syllables		number of vowels seen	vowels heard	syllables
1. grain				**13.** seedling			
2. rainbow				**14.** sailboat			
3. pie				**15.** toes			
4. deal				**16.** snowflake			
5. teacher				**17.** today			
6. paintbrush				**18.** feet			
7. train				**19.** oatmeal			
8. soak				**20.** three			
9. seal				**21.** tray			
10. raincoat				**22.** wheelchair			
11. may				**23.** coast			
12. tie				**24.** feeder			

Vowel Digraphs

Directions: Write each word under the correct picture. Then circle the vowel digraph in each word.

RULE

In a **vowel digraph**, two vowels together can make a long or a short vowel sound, or have a special sound all their own. The vowel digraph **oo** stands for the vowel sound in *look* or *cool*. The vowel digraph **ea** can stand for the short **e** sound you hear in *head*.

---

books	bloom	tooth	head
moose	bread	cook	weather
hood	dead	pool	wood

1.
_____

2.
_____

3.
_____

4.
_____

5.
_____

6.
_____

7.
_____

8.
_____

9.
_____

10.
_____

11.
_____

12.
_____

Vowel Digraphs

Directions: Read the clues to complete the crossword puzzles.

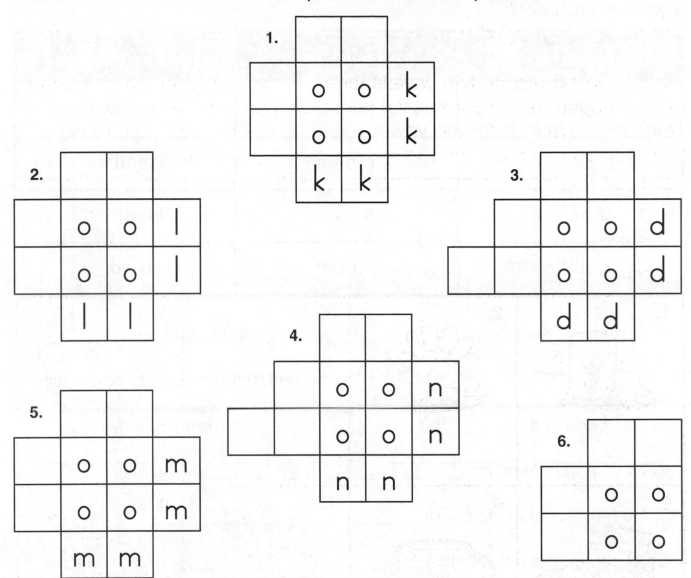

Set 1	Set 2	Set 3
• something to read	• a place to swim	• you wear it on your head
• hang your coat on this	• not warm	• logs that can be burned
• to fix food on the stove	• a hammer is this	• opposite of bad
• to see or use your eyes	• to trick someone	• stand up
Set 4	**Set 5**	**Set 6**
• 12:00	• to go fast	• animals live here
• shines at night	• a bomb makes this sound	• a ghost says this
• right away	• your bed is in here	• the sound a cow makes
• you eat with it	• unhappy fate	• also

Vowel Digraphs

Directions: Choose the word that will complete the sentence. Write it on the line.

oo as in cook	oo as in cool	ea as in head
brook	moose	breakfast
shook	groom	weather
cookies	stool	leather
crook	broom	bread

1. Please put the _____ in the toaster.

2. I _____ the present, but I couldn't hear anything!

3. The bride and _____ are ready to leave.

4. I like to eat cereal for _____ .

5. He has a coat made out of _____ .

6. Sweep up the dirt with this _____ .

7. We are going to make chocolate chip _____ .

8. I saw a _____ in the woods.

9. The _____ stole her jewelry.

10. What is the _____ like today?

11. We had a picnic in the woods by a _____ .

12. Here is a _____ to sit on.

Vowel Digraphs

Directions: Write each word under the correct picture. Then circle the vowel digraph in each word.

RULE

In a **vowel digraph**, two vowels together can make a long or a short vowel sound, or have a special sound all their own. The vowel digraphs **aw** and **au** stand for the vowel sound in *saw* and *haul*. The vowel digraph **ei** can have the long **a** sound as in *eight*.

| straw | eighteen | yawn |
| reindeer | August | sleigh |

| 1.
 _____ | 2.
 _____ | 3.
 _____ |
| 4. AUGUST
 _____ | 5. 18
 _____ | 6.
 _____ |

Directions: Choose a word to complete a sentence. Write it on the line.

saw   awesome   caught   eight   August   neighbors

7. I have a favorite memory from last _____ .

8. I _____ a baseball game with my dad.

9. Our next door _____ came with us.

10. We sat in row _____ .

11. I _____ a ball!

12. I had an _____ day!

Vowel Digraphs

Directions: Read each word. Write its vowel digraph on the line beside it.

1. caw _____
2. haul _____
3. eight _____
4. pause _____
5. paws _____
6. vein _____
7. freight _____
8. fawn _____

9. crawl _____
10. because _____
11. autumn _____
12. weight _____
13. flaw _____
14. law _____
15. maul _____
16. neighbor _____

17. eighteen _____
18. hawk _____
19. drawl _____
20. reindeer _____
21. squawk _____
22. cause _____
23. sleigh _____
24. claw _____

Directions: Use some of the words listed above to write four sentences of your own.

_____

_____

_____

_____

_____

Vowel Digraphs

Directions: Read each word. Write the number of syllables in the box beside the word. Find the meaning of the word and write that letter on the line after the word.

☐ haunted _____		**a.** number after seven
☐ vein _____		**b.** a month
☐ gawk _____		**c.** to carry
☐ reindeer _____		**d.** to look or stare
☐ brawny _____		**e.** lives next door
☐ pawn _____		**f.** after seventeen
☐ awesome _____		**g.** to catch or take
☐ eight _____		**h.** baby deer
☐ weight _____		**i.** Santa's animals
☐ August _____		**j.** strong
☐ neighbor _____		**k.** great, unbelievable
☐ fawn _____		**l.** spooky
☐ haul _____		**m.** carries blood
☐ eighteen _____		**n.** chess piece
☐ caught _____		**o.** amount of heaviness

Diphthongs

Directions: Write each word under the correct picture. Then circle the diphthong in each word.

RULE
In a **diphthong**, two vowels blend together to make one sound. The diphthongs **oi** and **oy** stand for the vowel sound in *toy* and *toil*. The diphthongs **ow** and **ou** stand for the vowel sound in *cow* and *mouse*. The diphthong **ew** stands for the vowel sound in *new*.

towel	mouse	owl	stew
hound	toys	jewels	soil
mew	foil	mouth	boy

1.	2.	3.	4.
_____	_____	_____	_____

5.	6.	7.	8.
_____	_____	_____	_____

9.	10.	11.	12.
_____	_____	_____	_____

Diphthongs

Directions: Read the words in the first column that describe the item. Look in the second column for a rhyming word. Print the answer in the third column.

Clue	Rhyme	Answer
you do this with gum	rhymes with crew	1. _____
silly person in a circus	rhymes with gown	2. _____
opposite of a girl	rhymes with toy	3. _____
opposite of north	rhymes with mouth	4. _____
not old	rhymes with flew	5. _____
a penny or a dime	rhymes with join	6. _____
a small city	rhymes with crown	7. _____
things to play with	rhymes with boys	8. _____
a circle is this shape	rhymes with pound	9. _____
dirt	rhymes with foil	10. _____
a pretty bloom	rhymes with shower	11. _____
a place to live	rhymes with mouse	12. _____
loud sounds	rhymes with poise	13. _____
what a kitten says	rhymes with dew	14. _____

Diphthongs

Directions: Use the words in the box to complete the story.

boy	town	house	noise	round	crowd
grew	proud	loud	Roy	ground	newspaper
join	cowboys	enjoy	choice	clown	threw

Can you hear the _____ ? That _____
                                      1   2

sound is coming from the fairground. A _____ is gathering
                                                      3

because the rodeo is in _____ !
                                4

I read about one of the _____ in the _____ .
                                  5   6

His name is _____ . He learned to ride a horse when he was
                     7

a _____ . After he _____ up, it was
                     8   9

his _____ to be a cowboy.
                 10

Yesterday in the first _____ of the rodeo, Roy was
                                      11

the fastest. He roped a calf and _____ it down on the
                                         12

_____ . He must have been _____ !
             13   14

Now he will _____ the other winners for the second
                           15

round of the rodeo.

Everyone in my _____ is going to the rodeo today.
                               16

We want to watch Roy and see the rodeo _____ .
                                            17

I know we will _____ our day at the rodeo!
                         18

Diphthongs

Directions: Underline every word with a diphthong. Then, write it in the correct box at the bottom of the page.

- Don't make a sound! I think I heard a mouse.
- I will line the pan with foil before I broil the steak.
- Do you think Joy will like this toy?
- As the wind blew, the bird flew away.
- You will need a towel after you take a shower.
- The dog barked, "Bow wow!"
- He is going to plow this piece of ground.
- The hound made a lot of noise.
- Come join my work crew!
- Joyce grew three inches.
- That boy is spoiled!
- I hope you enjoy your new house.

ou as in mouth	ow as in cow	oi as in oil	oy as in boy	ew as in few

Diphthongs

Directions: Count the syllables in each word. Write the word in the correct column.

flowerpot	boy	point	cowboy	showering
outside	jewelry	naughty	found	boiling
newspaper	flew	pow	prowler	spoil
royalty	noisy	powerful	mewing	cloudiness
threw	sound	enjoying	downtown	

1-Syllable Words	2-Syllable Words	3-Syllable Words

Unit Review

Directions: Read each word. Write a word on the line that has the same vowel spelling and the same vowel sound.

down   _____

drew   _____

soil   _____

sleigh   _____

raw   _____

boo   _____

hook   _____

dead   _____

goat   _____

knee   _____

jail   _____

pie   _____

cloud   _____

toy   _____

grow   _____

seed   _____

Unit Review

Directions: Name the picture. Circle every word in the row that has the same vowel sound.

1.	**fawn**	caught	blow	join
	crawl	batch	pause	raw
2.	**spoon**	book	crew	school
	threw	broom	shook	took
3.	**tree**	dream	thread	ten
	beam	sweater	speed	peach
4.	**toys**	tools	choice	boat
	boys	soil	enjoy	hay
5.	**mouse**	mice	blow	crowd
	shower	blouse	found	show
6.	**boat**	row	gloat	cot
	doe	mow	cow	toe
7.	**train**	eight	day	track
	stay	watch	paid	freight
8.	**pie**	pick	tie	lip
	tried	lie	miss	die
9.	**bread**	head	leather	mean
	ahead	team	ready	stream
10.	**hook**	cookie	wood	fool
	rookie	loose	book	stool

Unit Review

Directions: Underline the pair of letters working together to make the vowel sound. Then, write the word in the correct column.

goose	boat	cloud	joy
chain	street	rejoice	show
eight	law	heavy	ploy
look	author	sleigh	chew
leaf	voice	dream	saw
pool	snow	down	lie
treasure	town	today	
flew	foe	south	

Vowel Pairs	Vowel Digraphs	Diphthongs

Unit Review

Directions: Read each clue. Write its answer on the line beside it. Then, count the number of syllables in the answer and write that number in the next box.

woodpecker   noisy   join   shout   dawn

reindeer   annoy   pool   rainbow   newspaper

rowboat   down   weather   neighborly

Clue	Answer	Syllables
1. appears after it rains		
2. opposite of up		
3. pull Santa's sleigh		
4. a place for swimming		
5. a bird		
6. to put things together		
7. friendly and live close by		
8. reports daily events		
9. loud sounds		
10. beginning of the day		
11. uses oars to move on water		
12. to bother		
13. sunny, rainy, or cloudy		
14. to yell		

Unit Review

Directions: Complete each sentence with a word from the box.

autumn	moon	soap	stream	voice	headlines
drain	neigh	growl	snow	crawl	sweep
oyster	tray	Scout	cookies	screwdriver	
toe	tie				

1. If you go outside at night, you can see the _____ .

2. The ring slipped off my finger and went down the _____ .

3. The baby can't walk, but she can _____ .

4. An _____ lives in the ocean.

5. I like to read the _____ in the newspaper.

6. My brother is a Boy _____ .

7. I like to play in the _____ .

8. We made chocolate chip _____ .

9. I love the leaves in _____ !

10. I gave my dad a shirt and a _____ .

11. I put all of the food on a _____ .

12. I heard a horse _____ .

13. Be sure to wash your hands with _____ .

14. I dropped a brick on my _____ .

15. Listen to her sing. She has a beautiful _____ .

16. Take this broom and _____ the floor.

17. She heard the bear _____ .

18. We had a picnic by the _____ .

19. He just bought a hammer and a _____ .

Unit Review

Directions: Read the words in each row. Circle two words in the second box that have the same vowel sound as the word in the first box.

1. join	boy	boat	boil
2. mail	hat	hay	sailor
3. threw	screw	knew	know
4. frown	snow	pound	prowl
5. instead	ready	hen	leaves
6. cause	paw	cane	laundry
7. soy	voice	say	coy
8. grow	brown	throw	coal
9. shout	cloudy	cow	coat
10. eight	rain	bread	reindeer
11. room	zoom	lagoon	book
12. beach	great	green	cream
13. shook	crook	too	took
14. dawn	lawn	pause	rain
15. feet	seat	head	tree
16. moat	shout	hoe	soap

Unit Review

Directions: Use the words to complete the story.

ready	play	tea	lawn	cooks	row	rainy	fountain
queen	main	cloudy	coaches	reign	royal	join	awesome
noon	new	crowd	pie	Joe	because	crown	

Look at the _____ ! The people have gathered to read the
_____ decree. The _____ has declared a
holiday. She plans to celebrate the 50th year of her _____ .

The celebration will begin at _____ . The weather should be
perfect, not _____ or _____ . The queen's band
will _____ . Everyone will sit on the _____ .
The _____ will serve _____ and
_____ .

The celebration will continue with a dinner and a ball. Everyone will hurry to
get _____ . A _____ of punch will be
placed in the _____ ballroom. The queen will wear her gold
_____ and a _____ gown.

Many people will _____ the queen at her ball. Some will
arrive in _____ . Her son, Prince _____ ,
will _____ across the lake to attend the ball.

This celebration will be recorded in history _____ the
queen is the first to rule for 50 years. This is an _____ event
in my country!

UNIT 6
Prefixes, Base Words, Suffixes, and Syllables

124

Prefixes un–, dis–, and mis–

Directions: A **prefix** is a word part that is added at the beginning of a base word to change the base word's meaning or the way it is used. *Displeased* means not pleased. *Unsnapped* means not snapped. *Misuse* means used incorrectly. Read each word and write its base word on the line.

1. unfair _____

2. distaste _____

3. mistake _____

4. undo _____

5. undeserving _____

6. misread _____

7. uncoil _____

8. unworthy _____

9. unfinished _____

10. unkind _____

11. disconnect _____

12. undone _____

13. untrue _____

14. discolor _____

15. uncover _____

16. unbuckle _____

17. dislike _____

18. misjudge _____

19. misfit _____

20. misguide _____

Directions: Read each sentence. Write a word that means the same as the underlined words in the sentence.

21. The poor dog was <u>being treated badly</u>. _____

22. The dress was very <u>altered in color</u>. _____

23. The important papers were <u>put in the wrong place</u>. _____

24. The word was <u>not spelled correctly</u>. _____

25. The boy had his shoelaces <u>free from restraint</u>. _____

Prefixes ex–, de–, and re–

Directions: The prefix **re–** usually means do again. *Redo* means do again. The prefix **de–** usually means from. *Deport* means send away from. The prefix **ex–** usually means out of or former. *Export* means send out of. Read each word and write its base word on the line.

1. debug _____

2. reinstate _____

3. redo _____

4. expel _____

5. deplane _____

6. react _____

7. dehorn _____

8. exchange _____

9. exhale _____

10. refill _____

11. recharge _____

12. defrost _____

13. exclaim _____

14. defog _____

15. redefine _____

16. reclose _____

17. defuse _____

18. export _____

19. deploy _____

20. express _____

Directions: Fill in the circle beside the word that completes each sentence. Write the word on the line.

21. The wheat is an _____ to Russia.	◯ exchange	◯ export
22. The windows need to be _____ .	◯ deployed	◯ defrosted
23. We need to _____ the bull.	◯ detain	◯ dehorn
24. We need to _____ our computer.	◯ defuse	◯ debug
25. I want to have a _____ of my drink.	◯ reload	◯ refill

Prefixes Review

Directions: Read each sentence below. Write the word that best completes each sentence. Write the word on the line and complete the puzzle.

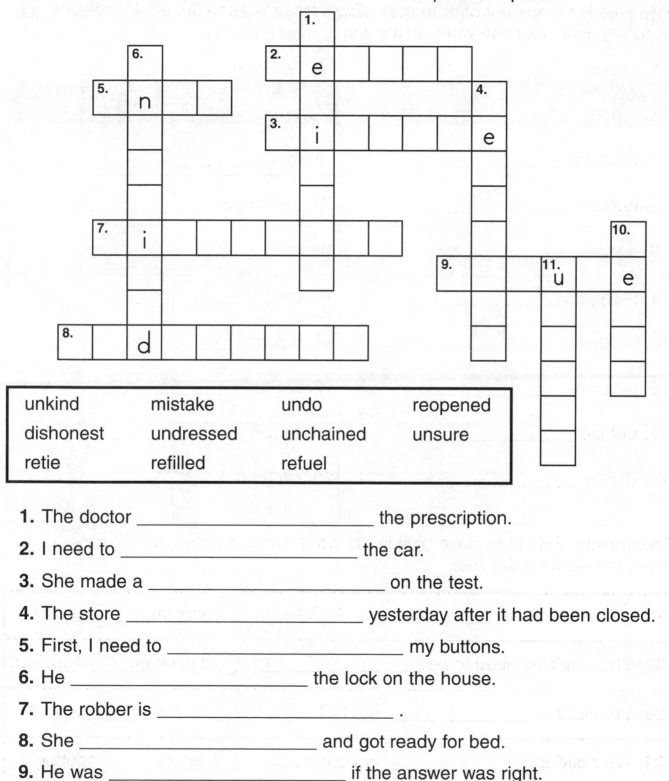

unkind   mistake   undo   reopened

dishonest   undressed   unchained   unsure

retie   refilled   refuel

1. The doctor _____ the prescription.

2. I need to _____ the car.

3. She made a _____ on the test.

4. The store _____ yesterday after it had been closed.

5. First, I need to _____ my buttons.

6. He _____ the lock on the house.

7. The robber is _____ .

8. She _____ and got ready for bed.

9. He was _____ if the answer was right.

10. He needs to _____ his shoes.

11. He is very _____ to me.

Prefixes, Base Words, and Suffixes

Directions: A **base word** is a word to which a prefix or a suffix may be added to form a new word. A **prefix** is added at the beginning of a base word. A **suffix** is added at the end of a base word. Read each word below and write its prefix, its base word, and its suffix in the correct columns.

Word	Prefix	Base Word	Suffix
1. reloaded			
2. refilled			
3. displeased			
4. dislocated			
5. mistaken			
6. discovered			
7. unplugged			
8. departing			
9. disobeying			
10. exporting			
11. dethroned			
12. misspelled			
13. disagreeable			
14. reopening			

Prefixes, Base Words, and Suffixes

Directions: Use the code to make the words below. Write the word on the line and circle the base word in each of the coded words.

a = 12	f = 19	k = 23	p = 15	u = 10
b = 5	g = 6	l = 7	q = 24	v = 25
c = 8	h = 21	m = 13	r = 2	w = 14
d = 4	i = 3	n = 9	s = 16	x = 11
e = 1	j = 22	o = 18	t = 17	y = 20

re(build)ing

1. _ _ _ _ _ _ _ _ _ _
2 1 5 10 3 7 4 3 9 6   _____

2. _ _ _ _ _ _ _ _ _ _
1 11 8 7 12 3 13 3 9 6   _____

3. _ _ _ _ _ _ _ _ _
10 9 14 2 12 15 15 1 4   _____

4. _ _ _ _ _ _ _ _ _ _ _ _ _
13 3 16 10 9 4 1 2 16 17 18 18 4   _____

5. _ _ _ _ _ _ _ _ _ _ _ _
10 9 8 18 13 19 18 2 17 12 5 7 1   _____

6. _ _ _ _ _ _ _ _ _ _ _
4 3 16 12 6 2 1 1 12 5 7 1   _____

7. _ _ _ _ _ _ _ _ _
8 12 2 1 19 10 7 7 20   _____

8. _ _ _ _ _ _ _ _ _ _ _
10 9 21 12 15 15 3 9 1 16 16   _____

9. _ _ _ _ _ _ _ _
2 1 18 15 1 9 1 4   _____

10. _ _ _ _ _ _ _ _
10 9 14 3 16 1 7 20   _____

Syllables: Prefixes and Suffixes

Directions: Divide a word with a prefix or suffix between the prefix or suffix and the base word. Use a hyphen (-) to divide the word. (Example: un-friend-ly) Divide each word below into syllables. Remember to use hyphens.

1. displease _____	**2.** distaste _____
3. undo _____	**4.** quickly _____
5. exclaim _____	**6.** calmness _____
7. remove _____	**8.** rewrote _____
9. repainted _____	**10.** disown _____
11. retake _____	**12.** owner _____
13. disagree _____	**14.** watches _____
15. unjust _____	**16.** walking _____
17. misspell _____	**18.** preview _____
19. miscounted _____	**20.** preheating _____
21. misplace _____	**22.** careful _____
23. unkind _____	**24.** unwise _____
25. softly _____	**26.** darkness _____
27. disclose _____	**28.** useless _____
29. untie _____	**30.** unpacking _____

Syllables: Prefixes and Suffixes

Directions: A **suffix** is a syllable if it contains a vowel sound. A **prefix** is always a syllable. (Examples: church-es, shoes, un-like) Read the divided words. Print the whole word on the line.

1. dis-taste-ful _____

2. re-paint-ing _____

3. mis-trust-ed _____

4. care-less-ness _____

5. re-plant-ed _____

6. un-kind-ness _____

7. quick-ly _____

8. re-turn-ing _____

9. ex-port-ed _____

10. dis-own _____

11. un-kind _____

12. white-ness _____

Directions: Underline each word that has a prefix or a suffix. Write the word or words on the line, using hyphens to divide the word into syllables.

13. It is unlikely that Julie will go to school. _____

14. She has been very sickly. _____

15. A cold has made her very sleepless. _____

16. She is very tired each morning. _____

17. She is disheartened that she has to miss school. _____

18. She has many friends in her class that she misses. _____

19. Her teacher always shows her great kindness. _____

20. Maybe tomorrow will be the day she can return. _____

Syllables: Compound Words

Directions: A one-syllable word is never divided. (Example: cat) Divide a compound word between the words that make up the compound word. (Example: snow-man) Divide each compound word below into syllables using hyphens.

1. football _____	2. softball _____
3. pigpen _____	4. jigsaw _____
5. snowshoe _____	6. shoelace _____
7. playground_____	8. sandbar _____
9. clipboard _____	10. teapot _____
11. playdough _____	12. eyebrow _____
13. bedtime _____	14. handshake _____
15. nighttime _____	16. playpen _____
17. rainbow _____	18. snowflake _____
19. sunshine _____	20. flashlight _____
21. daylight _____	22. mailman _____

Compound Words: Reading and Writing

Directions: Read the following passage. Circle the compound words.

The railroad passed through Snowville, a small town. The town had only four stores—an ice cream shop, a barbershop, the railroad station, and Barney's Supersaver. Everyone in Snowville loved hotdogs and soda. So Barney's Supersaver sold plenty of soda and hotdogs, especially on a hot day with lots of sunshine! You might say Snowville is the hotdog and soda capital of Washburn county!

Directions: Write a story about your hometown. Use some of the compound words in the word box below.

| playground | sidewalk | highway | newspaper |
| driveway | hillside | doghouse | sailboat |

Syllables: Words with Suffixes

Directions: When a word has a suffix with a vowel sound in it, divide the word between the base word and suffix. Divide each word below into syllables using hyphens.

1. driving _____	2. boxes _____
3. sadness _____	4. walking _____
5. singing _____	6. quickly _____
7. kindness _____	8. fearless _____
9. smallest _____	10. spoonful _____
11. faster _____	12. madly _____
13. careful _____	14. bolder _____
15. loudest _____	16. moving _____
17. softly _____	18. looking _____
19. hopeless _____	20. cuter _____
21. snooping _____	22. handful _____
23. tighten _____	24. holding _____
25. dresses _____	26. playful _____
27. golfing _____	28. surfing _____
29. reading _____	30. pushes _____

Syllables: Words with Prefixes

Directions: When a word has a prefix, divide the word between the prefix and the base word. Divide each word below into syllables using hyphens.

1. redo _____	2. unkind _____
3. declaw _____	4. rebuild _____
5. deport _____	6. rewrite _____
7. unmade _____	8. dislike _____
9. deplane _____	10. rewrap _____
11. mistrust _____	12. misuse _____
13. export _____	14. dislike _____
15. retrain _____	16. unfold _____
17. displace _____	18. discharge _____
19. unchain _____	20. misplace _____
21. defrost _____	22. exclaim _____
23. discolor _____	24. debug _____
25. unwrap _____	26. extend _____
27. unwise _____	28. replant _____
29. untie _____	30. mislead _____

Syllables: Words with Suffixes and Prefixes

Directions: Divide the words into syllables using hyphens.

1. skillfully _____

2. retrained _____

3. untimely _____

4. requested _____

5. departed _____

6. repairing _____

7. unkindly _____

8. mistaken _____

9. returning _____

10. discolored _____

11. repainted _____

12. undresses _____

Directions: Read each sentence below. Choose from the words above to complete the sentence. Write it on the line.

13. George's house needs to be _____ tomorrow.

14. The paint was very _____ and old.

15. Sam _____ built the deck.

16. Steve is _____ the car in the garage.

17. Sally _____ that Jane be present at the play.

18. The dog needs to be _____ not to bark.

19. Terry has been treating Jake _____ at school.

20. He was _____ . Joe had pushed her down.

Syllables: Multi-syllabic Words

Directions: When two or more consonants come between two vowels in a word, the word is usually divided between the first two consonants. Write each word dividing it into syllables using hyphens.

1. common _____	2. cannon _____
3. balloon _____	4. rabbit _____
5. candy _____	6. mountain _____
7. matter _____	8. mitten _____
9. tractor _____	10. channel _____
11. butter _____	12. banjo _____
13. rootbeer _____	14. campground _____
15. children _____	16. better _____
17. pothole _____	18. village _____
19. batter _____	20. market _____
21. wisdom _____	22. letter _____
23. carry _____	24. concert _____
25. center _____	26. wetter _____
27. running _____	28. doctor _____
29. fountain _____	30. persist _____

Syllable Review

Rule 1: A one-syllable word is never divided.
Rule 2: Divide a compound word between the words that make up the compound word.
Rule 3: When a word has a suffix with a vowel sound in it, divide the word between the base word and the suffix.
Rule 4: When a word has a prefix, divide the word between the prefix and the base word.
Rule 5: When two or more consonants come between two vowels in a word, the word is usually divided between the first two consonants.

Directions: Review the syllabication rules above. Write each word, dividing it into syllables using hyphens. Write the number of the rule that you used to help you.

1. system _____ ☐

2. slowly _____ ☐

3. retie _____ ☐

4. sidewalk _____ ☐

5. sooner _____ ☐

6. market _____ ☐

7. carefully _____ ☐

8. mistake _____ ☐

9. playing _____ ☐

10. kite _____ ☐

11. horse _____ ☐

12. driveway _____ ☐

13. basket _____ ☐

14. grapefruit _____ ☐

15. displeased _____ ☐

16. banker _____ ☐

17. restful _____ ☐

18. road _____ ☐

19. stopping _____ ☐

20. speeding _____ ☐

21. park _____ ☐

22. misuse _____ ☐

23. wolves _____ ☐

24. icing _____ ☐

Syllables: VCV Words

Directions: When a single consonant comes between two vowels in a word, the word is usually divided after the consonant if the first vowel is short. Write each word dividing into syllables using hyphens.

1. lavish _____

2. civil _____

3. palace _____

4. body _____

5. finish _____

6. magic _____

7. lemon _____

8. river _____

9. travel _____

10. seven _____

Directions: Write a story using as many of the above words as you can.

_____
_____
_____
_____
_____
_____
_____
_____
_____
_____
_____

Syllables: Multi-syllabic Words

Directions: Use the code to make the words below. Write the word on the line and divide into syllables using hyphens.

a = 12	f = 19	k = 23	p = 15	u = 10
b = 5	g = 6	l = 7	q = 24	v = 25
c = 8	h = 21	m = 13	r = 2	w = 14
d = 4	i = 3	n = 9	s = 16	x = 11
e = 1	j = 22	o = 18	t = 17	y = 20

1. __ __ __ __ __ __ __ __ __
   17 1 7 1 15 21 18 9 1   tel-e-phone
   _____

2. __ __ __ __ __
   16 12 4 7 20
   _____

3. __ __ __ __ __ __ __ __ __ __
   5 12 16 23 1 17 5 12 7 7
   _____

4. __ __ __ __ __ __
   17 3 15 17 18 1
   _____

5. __ __ __ __ __ __
   14 12 3 17 1 4
   _____

6. __ __ __ __ __ __ __
   13 12 3 7 5 18 11
   _____

7. __ __ __ __ __ __ __ __
   16 14 3 13 13 3 9 6
   _____

8. __ __ __ __ __ __ __
   21 10 9 4 2 1 4
   _____

9. __ __ __ __ __ __ __
   5 12 16 21 19 10 7
   _____

10. __ __ __ __ __ __ __
    17 2 12 19 19 3 8
    _____

11. __ __ __ __ __ __
    9 12 15 23 3 9
    _____

12. __ __ __ __ __ __ __ __
    21 18 13 1 7 1 16 16
    _____

13. __ __ __ __ __ __ __
    17 12 7 7 1 16 17
    _____

Syllables: VCV Words

Directions: When a single consonant comes between two vowels in a word, the word is usually divided before the consonant if the first vowel is long. Write each word dividing into syllables using hyphens. Then find those words in the puzzle below.

1. begin _____

2. sofa _____

3. pilot _____

4. pillows _____

5. lasso _____

6. puppies _____

7. cried _____

8. babies _____

9. ladies _____

10. yellow _____

11. spider _____

12. lazy _____

13. cozy _____

14. paper _____

15. monkey _____

16. turkey _____

17. hotel _____

18. pupils _____

```
m  c  s  d  v  h  o  n  e  y  b  h  t  j  i
o  l  k  g  t  p  c  j  t  w  e  x  u  e  z
n  a  e  v  h  u  g  h  j  n  v  b  r  b  d
k  x  e  c  a  p  m  n  b  s  d  a  k  e  l
e  j  m  p  i  l  l  o  w  s  n  b  e  g  a
y  d  c  u  r  l  a  d  r  p  w  i  y  e  d
c  c  o  p  y  i  s  o  l  i  n  e  s  p  i
p  r  z  p  c  c  s  o  y  d  e  s  v  a  e
i  i  y  i  v  r  o  d  i  e  o  p  c  p  s
l  e  n  e  s  a  c  e  f  r  d  l  a  e  v
o  d  x  s  s  a  d  v  r  b  t  a  b  r  j
t  a  s  t  e  y  m  a  n  y  h  z  i  k  l
b  v  m  y  p  u  p  i  l  s  e  y  n  e  o
c  h  o  t  e  l  r  o  w  c  b  e  g  i  n
x  e  e  s  y  e  l  l  o  w  n  s  o  f  a
```

Syllables: Vowel Sounded Alone

Directions: When a vowel is sounded alone in a word, it forms a syllable by itself. Read each word and circle the vowel that is sounded by itself. Then write each word dividing into syllables using hyphens.

1. unit _____

2. disobeyed _____

3. ocean _____

4. alive _____

5. Mexico _____

6. open _____

7. uniform _____

8. decimals _____

9. population _____

10. paragraph _____

11. ago _____

12. again _____

13. amuse _____

14. elephant _____

15. able _____

16. habitation _____

17. graduate _____

18. apron _____

Directions: Write a story using as many of the above words as you can. Circle those words.

_____

- -

_____

_____

- -

_____

_____

- -

_____

_____

- -

_____

_____

- -

_____

_____

- -

_____

Syllables: Two Vowels Together

Directions: When two vowels come together in a word and are sounded separately, divide the word between the two vowels. Write each word dividing into syllables using hyphens.

1. boa _____

2. duet _____

3. poet _____

4. polio _____

5. duel _____

6. rodeo _____

7. radio _____

8. diet _____

9. idea _____

10. ruined _____

11. ideas _____

12. giants _____

13. creating _____

14. lioness _____

15. dieting _____

16. pioneers _____

17. fuel _____

18. folio _____

Directions: Write three sentences using as many of the above words you can use. Illustrate one sentence.

_____

_____

_____

_____

My Illustration

Syllables: Words with le

Directions: When a word ends in **le** preceded by a consonant, divide the word before that consonant. Unscramble each word below and write the word on the line. Then divide each word into syllables using hyphens.

1. bbbleu ___bubble___	bub-ble	simple
2. plesmi _____		apple
3. pelpa _____		table
4. kalen _____		able
5. dlmied _____		bubble
6. utetrl _____		uncle
7. prulep _____		little
8. eagln _____		middle
9. klipce _____		purple
10. cnule _____		needle
11. tlteil _____		ankle
12. belat _____		pickle
13. cmusle _____		muscle
14. blea _____		angle
15. caelts _____		castle
16. eeendl _____		turtle

144

Unit Review

Directions: Say and spell each word. Write the word under the correct heading where it belongs.

powerful	poem	lemon	spoonful	document
smallest	colder	dragon	fluid	model
create	tiny	usual	giant	finish
polio	visit	pioneer	palace	eternal
dial	wagon	robin	rewriting	idea
electric	odor	flying	unkindly	pyramid
paper	graduate	tiger	music	

Words with a single consonant between two vowels	Words with prefixes or suffixes

Words with two vowels together sounding separately	Words with a single vowel as a syllable

Unit Review

Directions: Read each clue. Fill in the circle next to the prefix or suffix that will make a new word from the underlined word. Write the new word on the line.

1. to <u>tie</u> again _____	○ un- ○ re- ○ -ful	**2.** not <u>happy</u> _____	○ -less ○ -ness ○ un-
3. not <u>honest</u> _____	○ un- ○ -less ○ dis-	**4.** not in the right <u>place</u> _____	○ un- ○ -est ○ mis-
5. to <u>paint</u> again _____	○ -ness ○ re- ○ mis-	**6.** not able to <u>sleep</u> _____	○ mis- ○ -less ○ -ness

Directions: Read each word below. Fill in the circle beside the correct syllable division.

7. radio	○ r-adio	○ ra-dio	○ ra-di-o
8. nimble	○ nimble	○ nim-ble	○ nimb-le
9. fluid	○ fluid	○ flu-id	○ fl-uid
10. pyramid	○ pyramid	○ pyr-a-mid	○ py-ra-mid
11. tiny	○ tiny	○ ti-ny	○ tin-y
12. lemon	○ lemon	○ lem-on	○ le-mon
13. hungry	○ hun-gry	○ hungry	○ hung-ry
14. doghouse	○ do-g-h-ouse	○ dog-house	○ dog-ho-use
15. renew	○ renew	○ re-new	○ ren-ew

Unit Review

Directions: Read each sentence below. Circle the word or words with a prefix or suffix.

1. The winter storm was very powerful.

2. The whiteness of the snow was very blinding.

3. The children were hoping to go outside to play.

4. They were anxious to make their new sleds useful.

5. Joe thought it would be unwise to ski down the hill alone.

6. Janet disliked the snow so she stayed inside.

7. Sam was displeased that Janet would not go out to play.

8. The dampness of the snow made Sally's feet wet.

9. The kids were playing a harmless game of snow tag.

10. The snowman would need to be rebuilt.

Directions: Change each word below into a new word by adding a suffix or prefix of your own. Write the new word on the line.

11. paint _____

12. agree _____

13. own _____

14. care _____

15. quick _____

16. friend _____

UNIT 7

Synonyms, Antonyms, Homonyms, and Dictionary Skills

Synonyms

Synonyms are words that have the same or almost the same meaning. For example, *little* and *small* have similar meanings.

Directions: Read the words in the first column. Find a synonym in the second column. Write its letter on the line of the matching word.

1. sad _____   a. freezing

2. shut _____   b. tired

3. noisy _____   c. grin

4. mad _____   d. scared

5. hot _____   e. close

6. cold _____   f. large

7. tiny _____   g. easy

8. huge _____   h. loud

9. fearful _____   i. unhappy

10. sleepy _____   j. small

11. hard _____   k. fast

12. swift _____   l. boiling

13. simple _____   m. angry

14. sick _____   n. difficult

15. smile _____   o. ill

Synonyms

Directions: Complete the sentences using words from the list below. Write a word that makes sense in the top sentence. Then complete the next sentence with a synonym. Write that word on the second line.

quietly	friends	present	beautiful	baby
attractive	store	buddies	pretty	gift
infant	silently	shop	handsome	

1. The two boys are _____ .

The two boys are _____ .

2. The _____ is starting to crawl.

The _____ is starting to crawl.

3. The class worked _____ .

The class worked _____ .

4. We will buy his present at a toy _____ .

We will buy his present at a toy _____ .

5. I am going to wrap my _____ .

I am going to wrap my _____ .

6. Her boyfriend is very _____ .

Her boyfriend is very _____ .

7. Your flowers are _____ .

Your flowers are _____ .

Antonyms

Antonyms are words that are opposite or almost opposite in meaning. For example, *up* is the opposite of *down*.

Directions: Read the word in the first box. Find its antonym in the row and circle it.

1. up	out	down
2. tall	big	short
3. clean	dirty	spotless
4. inside	outside	upstairs
5. buy	purchase	sell
6. win	tie	lose
7. night	evening	day
8. send	receive	give
9. right	left	write
10. yes	accept	no
11. stop	start	halt
12. right	correct	wrong
13. float	sink	swim
14. girl	boy	woman

Antonyms

Directions: Complete the sentences using words from the list below. Write a word that makes sense in the top sentence. Then complete the next sentence with an antonym. Write that word on the second line.

quiet	read	play	lost	hot
listen	mother	cold	speak	noisy
write	found	father	work	

1. The porridge was too _____ .

   The porridge was too _____ .

2. I am going to _____ a book.

   I am going to _____ a book.

3. My _____ is a doctor.

   My _____ is a doctor.

4. I am going to the meeting to _____ .

   I am going to the meeting to _____ .

5. She is going to _____ all day long.

   She is going to _____ all day long.

6. I _____ my watch.

   I _____ my watch.

7. Our baby is _____ !

   Our baby is _____ !

Homonyms

Directions: Circle the homonym that matches the picture.

Homonyms are words that sound alike, but have different spellings and meanings. For example, *meat* and *meet* are alike only in the way they sound.

1. Ty tie	**2.** blew blue	**3.** pail pale
4. won one	**5.** meet meat	**6.** mail male
7. be bee	**8.** rap wrap	**9.** bear bare
10. I eye	**11.** sail sale	**12.** ate eight

Homonyms

Directions: Complete the sentences. Write a word that makes sense in the top sentence. Then complete the next sentence with a homonym. Write the word on the second line.

sew	for	Write	tail	build
billed	sea	by	four	right
buy	so	tale	see	

1. My little sister is _____ years old.

   This present is _____ her.

2. Look over there and you will _____ the ocean.

   I have always wanted to wade in the _____ .

3. We are going to _____ a new house.

   The lumber company _____ us for wood and nails.

4. My mom will _____ my costume.

   She has made other clothes for me _____ I know it will fit.

5. I am going to _____ that lamp.

   I will put it _____ my favorite chair.

6. This is the _____ answer.

   _____ it on the blank.

7. I wrote a _____ about my dog!

   Whenever he hears it, he wags his _____ !

Synonyms, Antonyms, and Homonyms

Directions: For each group of words, draw a line from the word in the first column to a word in the second column.

Draw a line between the **synonyms**.

lift	glad	beautiful	buy
find	woods	large	pretty
happy	locate	purchase	correct
forest	raise	right	big

Draw a line between the **antonyms**.

asleep	something	high	lead
fat	go	light	low
come	thin	follow	country
nothing	awake	city	heavy

Draw a line between the **homonyms**.

beat	brake	oar	weight
fair	beet	steak	stake
made	fare	wait	weak
break	maid	week	or

Synonyms, Antonyms, and Homonyms

Directions: Circle the words that go with the picture.

Synonyms have almost the same meaning. Circle the two synonyms that go with the picture.

1.
ship
boat
car
auto

2.
gift
gold
purse
present

3.
store
sack
bag
shop

4.
ring
infant
rattle
baby

5.
play
store
road
shop

Antonyms have opposite meanings. Circle the word that goes with the picture. Then circle its antonym.

6.
stop
up
wait
down

7.
read
play
healthy
sick

8.
bloom
eat
bed
die

9.
black
sun
moon
stars

10.
write
play
read
sleep

Homonyms sound alike but have different spellings and meanings. Circle the correct homonym for each picture.

11.
stares
stairs

12.
deer
dear

13.
ring
wring

14.
knows
nose

15.
not
knot

Alphabetical Order

Directions: Use the first letter of each word to help you place the words in alphabetical order.

dinosaur	_____
fish	_____
zipper	_____
uncle	_____
apple	_____
muffin	_____
spider	_____
cookie	_____
panda	_____
water	_____
horse	_____
guitar	_____
violin	_____
bubbles	_____
eagle	_____
noodles	_____

Alphabetical Order

Directions: Put these lists in alphabetical order using the second or the third letter in the word.

Words in a dictionary are listed in alphabetical order. If the first letters of the words are the same, look at the second letter. If the first two letters are the same, look at the third letter.

Alphabetize each set using the second letter.

Set 1		Set 2	
pickle	_____	class	_____
pooch	_____	coddle	_____
plant	_____	catch	_____
paint	_____	church	_____
purse	_____	cup	_____
proud	_____	city	_____
peanut	_____	center	_____

Alphabetize each set using the third letter.

Set 3		Set 4	
spout	_____	thumb	_____
spring	_____	thread	_____
splash	_____	think	_____
spunky	_____	thank	_____
speed	_____	then	_____
sparkle	_____	thought	_____

Guide Words

Directions: Look at each set of guide words. Circle the words in each list that you would find on a page with those guide words.

Guide words appear at the top of each dictionary page. They tell you what the first and last words on the page are. All the words on the page are in alphabetical order between the guide words.

1. **cap • cot**	2. **dog • eel**	3. **black • block**
cent	dinner	blood
cattle	eagle	blade
creek	elephant	blue
city	duck	bleed
class	dome	blip

4. **hive • jeep**	5. **lap • lug**	6. **pet • potion**
jacks	lock	puppy
hat	little	play
hug	lunch	pen
juggle	letter	pot
hopeless	ladle	pitch

7. **match • mop**	8. **stand • stump**	9. **freak • frown**
milk	steel	frame
muscle	stamp	frock
meddle	stick	freckle
map	stay	frump
mock	stun	fresh

Guide Words

Directions: Write each word under the correct set of guide words.

twin   velvet   bus   wren   dice   ribbon

chip   sheep   band   nickel   doze   nanny

1.

apple • bench	shake • ship	van • violet

2.

bug • cent	recess • riddle	twig • twist

3.

mice • net	dentist • doctor	nest • number

4.

dish • duck	wrap • wrist	cherry • choke

Guide Words

Directions: Decide on which page of the dictionary each word would be found. Write the page number beside it.

kabob • kitchen 175	knee • light 179	limp • lunch 181

king _____	list _____	lemon _____
locksmith _____	kangaroo _____	live _____
library _____	kettle _____	knife _____
loan _____	lawyer _____	kennel _____
lifeguard _____	kind _____	loose _____

sack • sock 245	suds • tickle 248	tock • tuck 251

trade _____	sand _____	swamp _____
supper _____	tuba _____	shell _____
trunk _____	settle _____	ticket _____
table _____	torch _____	sift _____
scone _____	summer _____	touch _____

Guide Words

Directions: Look at each pair of guide words. Find the five words that would be on the same page as those guide words. Write them in the large box. Then write those words in alphabetical order on the lines in the smaller boxes.

bubble	number	fish	marbles	balloon
monkey	night	belt	float	noodle
money	boat	brick	none	maybe
funny	frog	might	foggy	nudge

baby • bug

fan • fuzzy

maid • mud

name • nurse

Dictionary Skills

Directions: Where would each word be in the dictionary? Using the hint below, place each word in the correct column.

> Dictionary words are listed in alphabetical order. You can find a word quickly is you think of the dictionary as having three parts: Beginning Letters (A–I), Middle Letters (J–Q), and Ending Letters (R–Z).

wound	snow	glow	mood	lawn	creep
laundry	yawn	handle	jump	family	silly
purple	morning	zipper	chimp	desert	unicorn
apple	tickle	vowel	koala	bowl	quarter
octagon	eagle	riddle	neigh	riot	igloo

Beginning (A-I)	Middle (J-Q)	End (R-Z)

Dictionary Skills

Directions: Check the Beginning, Middle, or End box to tell where in the dictionary each word that is underlined can be found.

Beginning (A-I)   **Middle (J-Q)**   **End (R-Z)**

	Beginning	Middle	End
1. I like to eat <u>candy</u> corn.			
2. My favorite animal at the zoo is the <u>zebra</u>.			
3. When I grow up, I want to be a <u>queen</u>!			
4. My <u>teacher</u> is nice.			
5. She is a beautiful <u>ballerina</u>.			
6. What do you need to do to stay <u>healthy</u>?			
7. What does a <u>jaguar</u> look like?			
8. There is a <u>skeleton</u> in my doctor's office.			
9. Where in the universe in <u>Neptune</u>?			
10. I like to learn about <u>dinosaurs</u>.			
11. He can ride a <u>unicycle</u>.			
12. I am learning to use a <u>microscope</u>.			

Dictionary Skills

Directions: In each row, decide if the word will come on the page listed, before it, or after it. Use what you know about the three parts of the dictionary. Write *before*, *on*, or *after* in the space provided.

This is the word you want to look up.	These are the guide words for the page you are on.	Does the word come before, on, or after this page?
1. antelope	**balloon • best**	
2. lagoon	**lady • lily**	
3. Stegosaurus	**number • odd**	
4. ocelot	**number • odd**	
5. pelican	**paint • pink**	
6. quiver	**sand • sock**	
7. scarlet	**sand • sock**	
8. halo	**balloon • best**	
9. cobalt	**ant • apple**	
10. deuce	**dance • debt**	
11. aphid	**dance • debt**	
12. hemisphere	**gallon • hatch**	
13. Saturn	**rough • saw**	
14. trolley	**troop • trunk**	

Homographs

Directions: Read each dictionary entry. Underline the entry that goes with the picture.

Sometimes you will see two or more entry words in a dictionary that have different meanings but are spelled the same way. These words are called **homographs**.

1.	**pupil**[1]	A learner, one under the care of a teacher.
	pupil[2]	Opening in the iris of the eye.
2.	**skate**[1]	A fellow.
	skate[2]	Any of various rays having large pectoral fins.
	skate[3]	A boot or shoe fitted with a metal runner.
3.	**rocket**[1]	A firework or missle.
	rocket[2]	An herb.
4.	**hawk**[1]	A bird of prey.
	hawk[2]	To call out for the sale of goods in the street.
	hawk[3]	A small board used to hold plaster.
5.	**bear**[1]	To carry.
	bear[2]	Barley.
	bear[3]	A large mammal with a furry body and short tail.
6.	**bowl**[1]	To roll a ball.
	bowl[2]	A concave dish, larger than a cup.
7.	**rock**[1]	A mass of stone.
	rock[2]	To move back and forth.
8.	**punch**[1]	To strike or hit.
	punch[2]	A sweetened drink.
	punch[3]	A tool for indenting.

Homographs

Directions: Read the two definitions, and then read the sentence. Decide which definition fits the sentence and write its number in the box.

rift[1]	a disagreement between friends	
rift[2]	a shallow place in a stream	
1. What caused the <u>rift</u> between Joe and John?		☐

fly[1]	to move through the air on wings	
fly[2]	a small insect	
2. That <u>fly</u> has been bothering us.		☐

bank[1]	a steep slope or rising ground	
bank[2]	a place for safeguarding and lending money	
3. I am going to deposit my paycheck in the <u>bank</u>.		☐

corn[1]	a tall plant bearing seeds on a large ear or cob	
corn[2]	a thickening of skin, commonly on a toe	
4. My favorite vegetable is <u>corn</u>.		☐

kind[1]	a type or variety	
kind[2]	gentle and considerate behavior	
5. My grandmother is <u>kind</u> to everyone.		☐

drum[1]	a hill	
drum[2]	a percussion instrument	
6. He likes to play the bass <u>drum</u> in the band.		☐

lie[1]	an untrue statement	
lie[2]	to be in a recumbent position	
7. He is in trouble because he told a <u>lie</u>.		☐

Unit Review

Directions: Find the answer for each word. Write it on the line.

SYNONYMS

feeble	purchase
correct	dispatched

right_____

sent _____

weak_____

buy _____

ANTONYMS

sell	received
strong	wrong

right_____

sent _____

weak_____

buy _____

HOMONYMS

cent	write
by	week

right_____

sent _____

weak_____

buy _____

Unit Review

Directions: Read each sentence. Choose the meaning of the word that goes with the sentence. Write the number of the meaning beside the sentence.

dab[1]	a flatish
dab[2]	an expert
dab[3]	a little bit
grab[1]	to grasp or seize suddenly or forcibly
grab[2]	a vessel with two or three masts and a triangular sail
hoot[1]	a small amount, a bit
hoot[2]	the cry of an owl
leave[1]	to go or depart
leave[2]	official permission to be absent from duty
leave[3]	to put forth leaves
minute[1]	the 60th part of an hour
minute[2]	very small, tiny
rare[1]	infrequent in occurrence, uncommon
rare[2]	not completely cooked
shore[1]	coast or land next to a sea or river
shore[2]	to prop

_____ My brother is home on <u>leave</u> from the army.

_____ We are going to the <u>shore</u> for our vacation.

_____ Rub a <u>dab</u> of sunscreen on your nose.

_____ This steak is very <u>rare</u>.

_____ I will try to <u>grab</u> your balloon if you let go of it.

_____ Give me another <u>minute</u>, and I will be ready.

_____ We got scared when we heard a <u>hoot</u>.

Unit Review

Directions: Look at each pair of words. Put an X under the correct heading.

	Synonym	Antonym	Homonym
1. find – discover			
2. slowly – quickly			
3. whole – hole			
4. no – know			
5. fix – repair			
6. hear – here			
7. over – under			
8. to – too			
9. creep – crawl			
10. warm – cool			

Directions: Choose the correct word to complete the sentence.

pail   pale   blue   blew   male   mail   bear   bare

11. The wind _____ all night long.

12. I saw a _____ at the zoo.

13. I am going to _____ a card to my grandma.

14. Fill this _____ with water.

15. I won a _____ ribbon.

16. He has been sick and still looks a little _____ .

Unit Review

Directions: Put the words in alphabetical order.

brick	**1.**
black	**2.**
butter	**3.**
blue	**4.**
batter	**5.**
brown	**6.**
bonnet	**7.**
basket	**8.**

Directions: In each row, circle the guide words that would be at the top of a dictionary page for the bolded word.

9. deal	day – dead	deaf – dear	ditto – dive
10. flight	flick – flirt	flea – flier	flop – focus
11. giant	get – ghetto	gain – gap	ghost – gift
12. lanyard	lantern – lap	land – lank	leap – lee
13. mink	mint – minus	mine – minnow	monk – money
14. permit	pet – petty	perk – persist	peach – pedal
15. rate	rap – rash	rave – red	rasp – rating
16. safe	saber – sack	seed – sell	sad – sail

Answer Key

Answer Key

Page 5
1. b   5. s   9. t
2. p   6. g   10. k
3. l   7. m   11. p
4. h   8. r   12. z

Page 6
Pictures will vary. Make sure the picture matches the corresponding beginning letter.

Page 7
1. trip   5. days
2. ship   6. fish
3. pack   7. dive
4. bag   8. fun

Page 8
k—cookies and baker
l—balloons and police
n—honey and money
p—zipper and puppy
t—mitten and kitten

Page 9
1. r   5. m   9. n
2. t   6. g   10. r
3. k   7. n   11. k
4. p   8. t or b   12. n

Page 10
1. lady   5. pony
2. city   6. limo
3. pretty   7. daisies
4. wedding   8. balloons

Page 11
1. l   7. b   12. l
2. g   8. k   13. d
3. p   9. r   14. g
4. v   10. t   15. l
5. n   11. n   16. d
6. s

Page 12
Answers will vary, but suggestions are listed below.
bus—Gus, pus, fuss
whale—pale, male, stale
drum—bum, gum, hum
crown—down, gown, town
chair—fair, hair, pair
sink—link, pink, wink
sheep—deep, keep, peep
bride—died, lied, cried
king—ring, sing, wing
knife—life, wife, strife
ship—dip, hip, lip
egg—beg, leg, peg
block—dock, lock, knock
dove—love, above, shove
bed—fed, led, Ted

Page 13
1. gift   5. cap
2. shop   6. box
3. bat   7. bag
4. ball   8. six

Page 14
j (beginning)
z (beginning)
m (beginning)
t (middle)
r (middle)
f (end)
s (end)
w (beginning)
v (end)
p (beginning)
h (beginning)
g (middle)
c (beginning)
n (end)
l (middle)
x (end)

Page 15
city—soft
candy—hard
coat—hard
pencil—soft

castle—hard
celery—soft
ice—soft
coins—hard
prince—soft
cub—hard
cymbals—soft
cookies—hard
doctor—hard
carriage—hard
police—soft
ceiling—soft

Page 16
Hard c: cake, cute, cub, coast, capital
Soft c: cymbal, cider, civil, ceiling, cell

Page 17
1st puzzle: cannon, cup, corn—hard c
2nd puzzle: cube, carry, cocoa—hard c
3rd puzzle: circle, cyclone, cinnamon—soft c

Page 18
Underline: once, Cinderella, ceilings, cellars, cinders, palace, mice, lace, danced, prince
Circle: cleaned, care, came, rescue, carriage, decorated, castle, cake, castle

Page 19
gondola—hard
giraffe—soft
dragon—hard
pledge—soft
giant—soft
judge—soft
goose—hard
gate—hard
carriage—soft
hug—hard
golf ball—hard
general—soft
game—hard
bridge—soft
gem—soft
guard—hard

Page 20
Hard g: gorilla, guppy, gap, guitar, gallon, gumdrop, gondola
Soft g: giraffe, genius, ginger, gym, gentle, gypsy, gerbil

Page 21
1st puzzle: gorilla, guitar, dragon—hard g
2nd puzzle: giraffe, gypsy, giant—soft g
3rd puzzle: gallop, guess, garden—hard g

Page 22
Underline: bridge, giant, huge, oranges, oranges, magic
Circle: gate, gate, garden, garden, dragon, guarding, growing, grand, garden, garden, green, grass

Page 23
1. mop 5. nip 8. sap
2. hop 6. nap 9. sad
3. top 7. rap 10. dad
4. tip

Page 24
s: summer, Missy, bus
d: duck, radio, band
l: lucky, balloon, quill
v: van, heaven, cave
g: game, wagon, wig
p: peacock, zipper, ramp

t: tick, butter, comet

Page 25

Page 26
d (first)   s (last)
n (middle)   p (first)
y (first)   b (middle)
r (last)   k (middle)
1. penguin   4. queen
2. yellow   5. seven
3. candy

Page 27
Circle goblet, gander, cope, cartoon, gold, cupcake, guess, cackle, candle, gum, garden
1. gerbil   4. Cindy
2. goblet   5. germ
3. candle   6. cartoon

Page 29
Color ham, rat, can, track, hat, cat, map, tack, flag, fan, hand.

Page 30
1. pig   5. pin
2. sick   6. whip
3. knit   7. pills
4. wig   8. fish
Answers may vary. Suggestions are listed below.
9. pig   14. lick
10. flip   15. pill
11. sick   16. fig
12. whip   17. pin
13. knit   18. knit

Page 31
1. rug   5. slug
2. jug   6. run
3. gum   7. duck
4. bus   8. bump
Circle Duck, Bud, duck, truck, bumpy, Bud, jumped, truck, fun, ducks, gum, Bud, running, ducks, fun, Bud's, lucky

Page 32
lump, lamp, limp
jug, jag, jig
bun, ban, bin
yuck, yack, yick
sunk, sank, sink
sup, sap, sip
hum, ham, him
rug, rag, rig
rum, ram, rim
but, bat, bit
Short a—had, sash, brat, flat, ban, cap, gash
Short i—fit, rip, pin, bin, sip, grit, sill, will, fit
Short u—bun, fun, sub, plug, slug, rug

Page 33
1. mop   7. dock
2. pond   8. sock
3. rock   9. knock
4. doghouse   10. pot
5. cot   11. clock
6. log   12. frog

Page 34
1. bed   5. bell
2. tent   6. elf
3. hen   7. vest
4. ten   8. desk
Circle sled, pest, rent, bell, vet, den, tell, head.

Page 35
Stories will vary. Check to see if words in the list are contained in the story.

Page 36
1. bet   10. fan
2. but   11. tan
3. bit   12. tin
4. bat   13. ton
5. ban   14. won
6. bun   15. win
7. bin   16. wit
8. fin   17. wet
9. fun   18. jet

Page 37
1. guest   8. strong
2. frog   9. trip
3. hog   10. hug
4. test   11. hung
5. cross   12. sum
6. flag   13. went
7. quit   14. flat
Sentences will vary. Make sure each sentence uses at least one of the scrambled words.

Page 38
1. rake   7. mail
2. cake   8. sail
3. grapes   9. snail
4. chain   10. game
5. plate   11. rain
6. snake   12. plane

Page 39
1. dice   7. lion
2. bride   8. tie
3. pine   9. ice
4. lighthouse   10. tiger
5. smile   11. knife
6. slide   12. pie

Page 40
1. June   5. tuba
2. Utah   6. tune
3. uniforms   7. duet
4. tube

Page 41
long u word—blue, tuba, cute, flute, fruit, tube, suit, tune
long a word—whale, brake, name, shake, shame, rain, cake, Spain, wail
long i word—pipe, bite, line, fine, mile, bride, mice, spine

Page 42

Sentences will vary. Make sure sentences contain long o words.

Page 43
Circle Pete, Detroit, He, He, green, feet, trees, Pete, Jean, seals, see,

eagles, Jean, She, teeth, Pete's, greet, each.
1. Detroit   5. seals
2. green   6. eagles
3. trees   7. lion
4. Jean   8. teeth

Page 44
The path should be as follows: poke, boat, reed, sweep, doe, meat, feet, road, steel, joke, cone, wheel, mean, hole, green, bean, gloat, spoke.

Page 45
Across
1. heat   10. lie
3. rain   12. meat
6. fleet   14. pine
8. cute   16. cone
Down
2. leap   9. June
4. cake   11. kite
5. nail   13. nine
7. deep   15. eel

Page 46
Letters will vary. Check to see if some of the long vowel words are contained in the letter.

Page 47
Long u—flute,
    Short u—cup
Long e—feet,
    Short e—bed
Long a—snake,
    Short a—cap
Long i—kite,
    Short i—ship
Long o—goat,
    Short o—pot

Page 48
Long a: crate, rain, came, game, brain, cane, rate
Short a: lad, chat, hand, rat, wham, can, span
Long i: pride, hive, wife, spine, slice
Short i: twill, spin, gift
Long o: broke, throat, hose
Short o: fog, dock, drop, spot, top
Long e: heel, weep, team, sweet, jeep
Short e: bell, wren
Long u: suit, flute, tune
Short u: hug, trump

Page 49
1. stop   11. pig
2. mice   12. let
3. sleet   13. tone
4. keep   14. ton
5. lake   15. got
6. quit   16. dug
7. goat   17. oat
8. flute   18. sad
9. flake   19. tune
10. snake   20. dike
Sentences will vary. Make sure one word from the boxes are used in each sentence.

Page 50
1. Circle: hope, goat
    Underline: stop, hop
2. Circle: bride, line
    Underline: grin, bid
3. Circle: game, rain
    Underline: bat, can
4. Circle: feet, leap
    Underline: rent, get
5. Circle: flute, fuel
    Underline: fun, bud
6. Circle: write, kite

Underline: ban, sand
7. pail (colored)
8. grapes (colored)
9. sleep (colored)
10. clock
11. duck
12. globe (colored)
13. tape
14. cope
15. rain
16. slide
17. cane
18. tube

Page 51
1. cake   9. hen
2. pie   10. dish
3. Gus   11. meat
4. hot   12. came
5. soap   13. kite
6. rag   14. fix
7. tuba   15. band
8. fed
Long and short vowel words will vary.

Page 53
1. popcorn
2. bluebird
3. sailboat
4. beehive
5. raincoat
6. bookcase
7. bedroom
8. skydive
9. starlight
10. starfish
11. teapot
12. birdseed
13. moonbeam
14. meatball
15. gingerbread
16. seagull
17. cupcake
18. sunflower

Page 54
1. water, fall
2. tree, top
3. sun, day
4. post, card
5. apple, sauce
6. pan, cake
7. sea, shell
8. hair, brush
9. cup, cake
10. neck, tie
11. pea, nuts
12. air, way

Page 55
1. 2   7. 1   13. 1
2. 2   8. 2   14. 2
3. 1   9. 1   15. 1
4. 2   10. 2   16. 1
5. 2   11. 1
6. 1   12. 1

Page 56
1. dress   12. clap
2. bride   13. glass
3. frog   14. clam
4. prince   15. stairs
5. crib   16. spill
6. grass   17. snow
7. truck   18. swim
8. flag   19. smile
9. plug   20. squirrel
10. blouse   21. skunk
11. slide

Page 57
r Blends: princess, crowd,

Answer Key

draw, pretzel, bride,
fruit, dream, track, grill
l Blends: glove, black,
clock, glue, flower,
flute, blanket, planet
s Blends: stamp, spider,
swish, ski, scarf, sneak,
squirrel

Page 58
1. brother 2. class
3. playground
4. students
5. slides or swings,
swings or slides
6. squirrels, trees
7. trip
8. blocks, planetarium
9. spoke
10. planets or stars, stars
or planets
11. studied
12. bridge
13. trucks/planes/trains
(any order)
14. dream

Page 59
1. bunk 9. rink
2. film 10. east
3. plant 11. list
4. bank 12. sink
5. sand 13. tank
6. camp 14. toast
7. nest 15. sling
8. vest 16. think

Page 60
1. dry, i
2. fry, i
3. fairy, e
4. sky, i
5. sunny, e
6. marry, e
7. jelly, e
8. candy, e
9. shy, i
10. cherry, e

Page 61
1. yak 4. yolk
2. yard 5. yo-yo
3. yacht 6. yarn
y as a consonant: yellow,
you, year, young, yell
y sound = long e: sorry,
hurry, pretty, many, buddy
y sound = long i: fry, sly,
sty, my, try

Page 62
1. Yesterday 12. butterfly
2. city 13. shy
3. sky 14. fly
4. puffy 15. Finally
5. windy 16. pretty
6. years 17. yellow
7. My 18. try
8. by 19. funny
9. dry 20. happy
10. empty 21. You
11. You 22. cry
                22. spy

Page 63
1. throne 8. whale
2. wrench 9. church
3. cherry 10. thimble
4. chain 11. ship
5. shark 12. wheel
6. thread 13. shuttle
7. sheep 14. knit

Page 64
1. church 9. wrist
2. ship 10. whale
3. gnaw 11. school
4. think 12. knot
5. wrist 13. think
6. whale 14. ship
7. knot 15. church
8. school 16. gnaw

Page 65
1. ch, middle
2. sh, beginning
3. th, middle
4. ch, end
5. ch, middle
6. ck, end
7. wh, beginning
8. kn, beginning
9. th, middle
10. sh, beginning
11. gh, end
12. gh, middle
13. gn, end
14. wh, beginning
15. wr, beginning

Page 66
1. sweater 7. parrot
2. yard 8. yogurt
3. flowers 9. mother
4. weather 10. ruler
5. giraffe 11. hammer
6. letters 12. spider

Page 67
1. birthday 10. purple
2. north 11. star
3. garden 12. nurse
4. hurry 13. horse
5. yesterday 14. thirteen
6. morning 15. sweater
7. circus 16. turkey
8. thunder 17. sister
9. candy bar 18. bird

Page 68
1. grandfather, farmer
2. corn
3. farm, summer
4. tractor
5. fertilizer
6. bigger
7. taller
8. hard
9. porch, guitar
10. party, barn
11. surprised
12. Saturday, river
13. working
14. turned, favorite

Page 69
1. turtle, batter,
hammer, 2
2. shirt, skirt, nurse, 1
3. dipper, cracker,
dollar, 2
4. Florida, celery,
computer, 3
5. letter, checkmark,
carrot, 2

Page 70
1 syllable: fry, wheat,
yam, wrote, know,
clock, wish, cry
2 syllables: dustpan,
dragon, ticket, yipee,
milkweed, candy, silly,
shower
3 syllables: telephone,
elephant, Saturday,
umbrella, chocolate,
computer, countertop,
yesterday

Page 71
1. 3, 2, 2 9. 2, 1, 1
2. 2, 1, 1 10. 2, 2, 2
3. 5, 3, 3 11. 3, 2, 2
4. 4, 4, 4 12. 2, 2, 2
5. 2, 2, 2 13. 3, 3, 3
6. 2, 1, 1 14. 2, 2, 2
7. 2, 1, 1 15. 2, 1, 1
8. 2, 1, 2 16. 3, 3, 3

Page 72
Down
1. crow 5. dirty
2. shy 7. plum
3. turtle 8. star
Across
1. chips 6. stamp
2. short 9. throne
4. under 10. yes

Page 73
Blends: drink, gruff,
smoke, frame, plane,
blue, stamp, clap
Digraphs: chimney, why,
wrap, thick, shop, tough,
know, south
R-Controlled Vowels:
curtain, girl, better, purse,
car, turkey, her, for

Page 74
1. 3, water, fall
2. 2, rail, road
3. 2, class, mate
4. 3, butter, fly
5. o, 1 19. cl
6. e, 2 20. br
7. a, 1 21. gr
8. a, 1 22. pl
9. u, 2 23. st
10. i, 1 24. tr
11. i, 2 25. kn
12. e, 2 26. wr
13. e, 2 27. sh
14. u, 1 28. ch
15. o, 1 29. wh
16. u, 1 30. th
17. mp 31. ck
18. fl 32. gn
Y as a Consonant:
yo-yo, yolk
Y = Long e Sound:
sandy, happy
Y = Long i Sound: Ty, shy

Page 75
1. July 14. school
2. third 15. party
3. backyard 16. try
4. treehouse 17. secret
5. decorated 18. chocolate
6. yellow 19. skywriter
7. smiled 20. telephone
8. gift 21. whisper
9. year 22. finishing
10. surprise 23. pretty
11. birthday 24. think
12. beach 25. What
13. friends

Page 77
1. There's, There is
2. hasn't, has not
3. There's, There is
4. I've, I have
5. What's, What is
6. He's, He is
7. We've, We have
8. hasn't, has not
9. doesn't, does not
10. We've, We have
11. They're, They are
12. couldn't, could not
13. Isn't, Is not
14. you've, you have
15. We'll, We will
16. There's, There is

Page 78
The following words
should be circled: I'll,
you'll, I'll, we'll, It's,
Let's, We're, don't,
We're, shouldn't, we're,
aren't, shouldn't, Let's,
Wouldn't
I will
you will
I will
we will
It is
Let us
We are
do not
We are
should not
we are
are not
should not
Let us
Would not

Page 79
1. houses (colored)
2. foxes (colored)
3. car
4. doll
5. crutches (colored)
6. dish
7. trumpets (colored)
8. bed
9. es 13. es
10. es 14. es
11. es 15. es
12. es 16. es

Page 80
1. flies 11. patch
2. enemies 12. sky
3. babies 13. boy
4. turkeys 14. puppy
5. cities 15. charity
6. donkeys 16. army
7. toys 17. story
8. ladies 18. monkey
9. rays 19. day
10. worries 20. joy

Page 81
1. knives 8. loaves
2. wolves 9. knives
3. hooves 10. calves
4. leaves 11. shelves
5. scarves 12. halves
6. calves 13. loaves
7. halves

Page 82
1. dresses, dressed,
dressing
2. jumps, jumped,
jumping
3. looks, looked, looking
4. washes, washed,
washing
5. walks, walked, walking
6. snack 11. park
7. cap 12. star
8. patch 13. house
9. fox 14. load
10. heat 15. cross
Sentences will vary.
Check to see if at least
three plural words are used.

Page 83
1. smarter 10. dancer
2. smallest 11. talker
3. funniest 12. skater
4. happiest 13. player
5. greatest 14. writer
6. scariest 15. walker
7. thirstiest 16. speaker
8. smartest 17. reader
9. preacher 18. watcher

Page 84
Stories will vary. Check
to see if words in plural
form are included.

Page 85
1. running 10. beg
2. hugged 11. pat
3. digging 12. hop
4. planning 13. sad
5. winning 14. stab
6. hitting 15. dig
7. shopping 16. slim
8. swimming 17. plan
9. sit 18. tap

Page 86
Stories will vary. Check
to see if at least five of
the silent e words with
the suffixes are used in
the story.

Page 87
1. walking 9. singing
2. hoping 10. swimming
3. reading 11. making
4. living 12. craving
5. reading 13. heading
6. smarter 14. happier
7. dancer 15. happiest
8. dancing

Page 88
1. hugging, hugged
2. dancing, danced
3. hopping, hopped
4. dragging, dragged
5. stunning, stunned
6. boxing, boxed
7. loved, love
8. shopping, shop
9. going, go
10. giving, give
11. happiest, happy
12. named, name
13. teacher, teach
14. teaching, teach

Page 89
1. alertness 6. helpful
2. careful 7. meekly
3. sickly 8. weakness
4. tasteless 9. watchful
5. darkness 10. lowly

Page 90
–ness: sadness, madness,
neatness, quickness, calmness
–less: careless, painless,
thankless, hopeless, aimless
–ly: carefully, brightly,
kindly, gladly, sickly
–er: sicker, smaller,
cuter, louder, helper, taller
–est: neatest, smallest,
greatest, smartest

Page 91
1. windy 9. spooky
2. crunchy 10. squeaky
3. snowy 11. rusty
4. rainy 12. windy
5. itchy 13. rainy
6. sleepy 14. scary
7. scary 15. freaky
8. messy

Page 92
1. tight 6. depend
2. loose 7. sweet
3. suit 8. move
4. love 9. measure
5. shake 10. name

Page 93
1. snowy, snow
2. stormy, storm
3. frosty, frost
4. fluffy, fluff
5. pointy, point
6. brighten, bright
7. darken, dark
8. straighten, straight
9. lighten, light
10. soften, soft
11. suitable, suit
12. likeable, like
13. lovable, love
14. readable, read
15. breakable, break

Page 94
1. walk/ing, walk-ing
2. grow/ing, grow-ing
3. bright/en, bright-en
4. wish/ful, wish-ful
5. cup/ful, cup-ful
6. sled/ding, sled-ding
7. sweet/ly, sweet-ly
8. crutch/es, crutch-es
9. want/ed, want-ed
10. writ/ing, writ-ing
11. help/ful, help-ful
12. paint/er, paint-er
13. cheer/y, cheer-y
14. rain/y, rain-y
15. sleep/y, sleep-y
16. dark/ness, dark-ness
17. spin/ning, spin-ning
18. quick/ly, quick-ly
19. tall/est, tall-est
20. help/less, help-less
21. small/er, small-er
22. wind/y, wind-y
23. run/ning, run-ning
24. light/en, light-en
25. sleep/ing, sleep-ing
26. whit/en, whit-en
27. harm/less, harm-less
28. branch/es, branch-es
29. skies, skies
30. blows, blows

Page 95
1. neatness 11. painting
2. breakable 12. waiting
3. cupful 13. helper
4. spoonful 14. earnest
5. sadly 15. smaller
6. teacher 16. worker
7. lucky 17. brightness
8. lighten 18. useless
9. darkness 19. cheerful
10. hopeless 20. snowy
Sentences will vary. Check
to see if some of the
words on the list were used.

Page 96
–s, –es: crutches,
watches, worries,
games, boxes, loves,
pens, makes, misses,
sheets
–ing, –er, –est, –ed:
dancing, bumped,
happier, seemed,
worried, jogging,
writing, tanning,
reading, wiper
–ly, –ful, –less, –ness:
wonderful, meekly,
careful, happiness,
harmless, hopeless,
gladly, brightness
–y, –en, –able: stoppable,
brighten, snowy,
whiten, pliable, scary,
darken

Page 97
Stories will vary. Check

Answer Key

to see if several words in the list were used.

Page 98
1. perform
2. parents
3. practicing
4. singing
5. helpful
6. decorations
7. snowflakes
8. carefully
9. boxes
10. biggest
11. We're
12. useless
13. I've
14. Darkness
15. Today's

Page 99
1. you'll
2. they're
3. I'm
4. couldn't
5. it's
6. he's
7. stories
8. boys
9. wolves
10. madly
11. quietness
12. tallest
13. jumped
14. hiding
15. tipping
16. useless
17. cuter
18. lumpy

Sentences will vary.
Check to see that at least one word with a suffix and a contraction are in each sentence.

Page 101
1. chain
2. goat
3. tie
4. teeth
5. teacher
6. sailboat
7. tray
8. toes
9. bowl
10. read
11. rowboat
12. pie

Page 102
1. stray
2. squeal
3. doe
4. rainbow
5. play
6. screamed
7. moat
8. stain
9. wreath
10. tie
11. float
12. blow
13. mail
14. jeans

Page 103
1. jeep
2. toe
3. slow
4. day
5. peach
6. coat
7. clean
8. tail
9. lie
10. brain

Page 104
1. Kay, train
2. Joe, beach
3. need, weed
4. Fay, hoe
5. rain, snow
6. flow, road
7. tree, green
8. eat, pie
9. main, fear
10. grow, die

Page 105
1. 2, 1, 1
2. 4, 2, 2
3. 2, 1, 1
4. 2, 1, 1
5. 3, 2, 2
6. 3, 2, 2
7. 2, 1, 1
8. 2, 1, 1
9. 2, 1, 1
10. 4, 2, 2
11. 2, 1, 1
12. 2, 1, 1
13. 3, 2, 2
14. 4, 2, 2
15. 2, 1, 1
16. 4, 2, 2
17. 3, 2, 2
18. 2, 1, 1
19. 4, 2, 2
20. 2, 1, 1
21. 2, 1, 1
22. 4, 2, 2
23. 2, 1, 1
24. 3, 2, 2

Page 106
1. dead
2. bloom
3. wood
4. bread
5. books
6. pool
7. weather
8. moose
9. hood
10. tooth
11. cook
12. head

Page 107
1. book, hook, cook, look
2. pool, cool, tool, fool
3. hood, wood, good, stood
4. noon, moon, soon, spoon
5. zoom, boom, room, doom
6. zoo, boo, moo, too

Page 108
1. bread
2. shook
3. groom
4. breakfast
5. leather
6. broom
7. cookies
8. moose
9. crook
10. weather
11. brook
12. stool

Page 109
1. sleigh
2. yawn
3. reindeer
4. August
5. eighteen
6. straw
7. August
8. saw
9. neighbors
10. eight
11. caught
12. awesome

Page 110
1. aw
2. au
3. ei
4. au
5. aw
6. ei
7. ei
8. aw
9. aw
10. au
11. au
12. ei
13. aw
14. aw
15. au
16. ei
17. ei
18. aw
19. aw
20. ei
21. aw
22. au
23. ei
24. aw

Sentences will vary.
Check to see if some of the words listed were included.

Page 111
2, haunted, l.
1, vein, m.
1, gawk, d.
2, reindeer, i.
2, brawny, j.
1, pawn, n.
2, awesome, k.
1, eight, a.
1, weight, o.
2, August, b.
2, neighbor, e.
1, fawn, h.
1, haul, c.
2, eighteen, f.
1, caught, g.

Page 112
1. foil
2. hound
3. jewels
4. owl
5. stew
6. towel
7. boy
8. mouse
9. mouth
10. soil
11. mew
12. toys

Page 113
1. chew
2. clown
3. boy
4. south
5. new
6. coin
7. town
8. toys
9. round
10. soil
11. flower
12. house
13. noise
14. mew

Page 114
1. noise
2. loud
3. crowd
4. town
5. cowboys
6. newspaper
7. Roy
8. boy
9. grew
10. choice
11. round
12. threw
13. ground
14. proud
15. join
16. house
17. clown
18. enjoy

Page 115
Underline: sound, mouse, foil, broil, Joy, toy, blew, flew, towel, shower, Bow, wow, plow, ground, hound, noise, join, crew, Joyce, grew, boy, spoiled, enjoy, new, house
ou—sound, mouse, ground, hound, house
ow—towel, shower, Bow, wow, plow
oi—foil, broil, noise, join, spoiled
oy—Joy, toy, Joyce, boy, enjoy
ew—blew, flew, crew, grew, new

Page 116
1–syllable words: threw, boy, flew, sound, point, pow, found, spoil
2–syllable words: outside, noisy, naughty, cowboy, prowler, mewing, downtown, boiling
3–syllable words: flowerpot, newspaper, royalty, jewelry, powerful, enjoying, showering, cloudiness

Page 117
Suggestions are listed below.
down/town   goat/coat
drew/threw   knee/free
soil/toil   jail/rail
sleigh/neigh pie/tie
raw/saw   cloud/house
boo/coo   toy/boy
hook/cook   grow/mow
dead/head   seed/need

Page 118
1. fawn, crawl, caught, pause, raw
2. spoon, threw, broom, crew, school
3. tree, beam, dream, speed, peach
4. toys, boys, soil, choice, enjoy
5. mouse, shower, blouse, found, crowd
6. boat, doe, row, mow, gloat, toe
7. train, stay, eight, day, paid, freight
8. pie, tried, lie, tie, die
9. bread, ahead, head, leather, ready
10. hook, rookie, cookie, wood, book

Page 119
Vowel Pairs: boat, chain, street, show, leaf, dream, snow, lie, today, foe
Vowel Digraphs: goose, eight, law, heavy, look, author, sleigh, saw, pool, treasure
Diphthongs: cloud, joy, rejoice, ploy, chew, voice, down, town, south, flew

Page 120
1. rainbow, 2
2. down, 1
3. reindeer, 2
4. pool, 1
5. woodpecker, 3
6. join, 1
7. neighborly, 3
8. newspaper, 3
9. noisy, 2
10. dawn, 1
11. rowboat, 2
12. annoy, 2
13. weather, 2
14. shout, 1

Page 121
1. moon
2. drain
3. crawl
4. oyster
5. headlines
6. Scout
7. snow
8. cookies
9. autumn
10. tie
11. tray
12. neigh
13. soap
14. toe
15. voice
16. sweep
17. growl
18. stream
19. screwdriver

Page 122
1. boy, boil
2. hay, sailor
3. screw, knew
4. pound, prowl
5. ready, hen
6. paw, laundry
7. voice, coy
8. throw, coal
9. cloudy, cow
10. rain, reindeer
11. zoom, lagoon
12. green, cream
13. crook, took
14. lawn, pause
15. seat, tree
16. hoe, soap

Page 123
1. crowd
2. royal
3. queen
4. reign
5. noon
6. rainy/cloudy
7. cloudy/rainy
8. play
9. lawn
10. cooks
11. tea/pie
12. pie/tea
13. ready
14. fountain
15. main
16. crown
17. new
18. join
19. coaches
20. Joe
21. row
22. because
23. awesome

Page 125
1. fair
2. taste
3. take
4. do
5. deserve
6. read
7. coil
8. worth
9. finish
10. kind
11. connect
12. done
13. true
14. color
15. cover
16. buckle
17. like
18. judge
19. fit
20. guide
21. mistreated
22. discolored
23. misplaced
24. misspelled
25. untied

Page 126
1. bug
2. state
3. do
4. pel
5. plane
6. act
7. horn
8. change
9. hale
10. fill
11. charge
12. frost
13. claim
14. fog
15. define
16. close
17. fuse
18. port
19. ploy
20. press
21. export
22. defrosted
23. dehorn
24. debug
25. refill

Page 127

1. refilled
2. refuel
3. mistake
4. reopened
5. undo
6. unchained
7. dishonest
8. undressed
9. unsure
10. retie
11. unkind

Page 128
1. re, load, ed
2. re, fill, ed
3. dis, please, ed
4. dis, locate, ed
5. mis, take, en
6. dis, cover, ed
7. un, plug, ed
8. de, part, ing
9. dis, obey, ing
10. ex, port, ing
11. de, throne, ed
12. mis, spell, ed
13. dis, agree, able
14. re, open, ing

Page 129
1. rebuilding
2. exclaiming
3. unwrapped
4. misunderstood
5. uncomfortable
6. disagreeable
7. carefully
8. unhappiness
9. reopened
10. unwisely

Page 130
1. dis-please
2. dis-taste
3. un-do
4. quick-ly
5. ex-claim
6. calm-ness
7. re-move
8. re-wrote
9. re-paint-ed
10. dis-own
11. re-take
12. own-er
13. dis-agree
14. watch-es
15. un-just
16. walk-ing
17. mis-spell
18. pre-view
19. mis-count-ed
20. pre-heat-ing
21. mis-place
22. care-ful
23. un-kind
24. un-wise
25. soft-ly
26. dark-ness
27. dis-close
28. use-less
29. un-tie
30. un-pack-ing

Page 131
1. distasteful
2. repainting
3. mistrusted
4. carelessness
5. replanted
6. unkindness
7. quickly
8. returning
9. exported
10. disown
11. unkind
12. whiteness
13. un-like-ly
14. sick-ly
15. sleep-less
16. tired
17. dis-heart-ened
18. miss-es
19. teach-er, kind-ness
20. re-turn

Page 132
1. foot-ball
2. soft-ball
3. pig-pen
4. jig-saw
5. snow-shoe
6. shoe-lace
7. play-ground
8. sand-bar
9. clip-board
10. tea-pot
11. play-dough
12. eye-brow
13. bed-time
14. hand-shake
15. night-time
16. play pen
17. rain-bow
18. snow-flake
19. sun-shine
20. flash-light
21. day-light
22. mail-man

Page 133
Circle railroad, Snowville, barbershop, railroad, Supersaver, Everyone, Snowville, hotdogs, Supersaver, hotdogs, sunshine, Snowville, hotdog, Washburn.
Stories will vary. Check to see if some of the compound words listed in the box are included.

Page 134
1. driv-ing
2. box-es
3. sad-ness
4. walk-ing
5. sing-ing
6. quick-ly
7. kind-ness
8. fear-less
9. small-est
10. spoon-ful
11. fast-er
12. mad-ly
13. care-ful
14. bold-er
15. loud-est
16. mov-ing
17. soft-ly
18. look-ing
19. hope-less
20. cut-er
21. snoop-ing
22. hand-ful
23. tight-en

Answer Key

24. hold-ing
25. dress-es
26. play-ful
27. golf-ing
28. surf-ing
29. read-ing
30. push-es

Page 135
1. re-do
2. un-kind
3. de-claw
4. re-build
5. de-port
6. re-write
7. un-made
8. dis-like
9. de-plane
10. re-wrap
11. mis-trust
12. mis-use
13. ex-port
14. dis-like
15. re-train
16. un-fold
17. dis-place
18. dis-charge
19. un-chain
20. mis-place
21. de-frost
22. ex-claim
23. dis-color
24. de-bug
25. un-wrap
26. ex-tend
27. un-wise
28. re-plant
29. un-tie
30. mis-lead

Page 136
1. skill-ful-ly
2. re-trained
3. un-time-ly
4. re-quest-ed
5. de-part-ed
6. re-pair-ing
7. un-kind-ly
8. mis-tak-en
9. re-turn-ing
10. dis-col-ored
11. re-paint-ed
12. un-dress-es
13. repainted
14. discolored
15. skillfully
16. repairing
17. requested
18. retrained
19. unkindly
20. mistaken

Page 137
1. com-mon
2. can-non
3. bal-loon
4. rab-bit
5. can-dy
6. moun-tain
7. mat-ter
8. mit-ten
9. trac-tor
10. chan-nel
11. but-ter
12. ban-jo
13. root-beer
14. camp-ground
15. chil-dren
16. bet-ter
17. pot-hole
18. vil-lage
19. bat-ter
20. mar-ket
21. wis-dom
22. let-ter
23. car-ry
24. con-cert

25. cen-ter
26. wet-ter
27. run-ning
28. doc-tor
29. foun-tain
30. per-sist

Page 138
1. sys-tem, 5
2. slow-ly, 3
3. re-tie, 4
4. side-walk, 2
5. soon-er, 3
6. mar-ket, 5
7. care-ful-ly, 3
8. mis-take, 4
9. play-ing, 3
10. kite, 1
11. horse, 1
12. drive-way, 2
13. bas-ket, 5
14. grape-fruit, 2
15. dis-pleased, 4
16. bank-er, 3
17. rest-ful, 3
18. road, 1
19. stop-ping, 5
20. speed-ing, 3
21. park, 1
22. mis-use, 4
23. wolves, 1
24. ic-ing, 3

Page 139
1. lav-ish   6. mag-ic
2. civ-il   7. lem-on
3. pal-ace   8. riv-er
4. bod-y   9. trav-el
5. fin-ish   10. sev-en
Stories will vary.
Check to see if some
of the words listed
are included.

Page 140
1. tel-e-phone
2. sad-ly
3. bas-ket-ball
4. tip-toe
5. wait-ed
6. mail-box
7. swim-ming
8. hun-dred
9. bash-ful
10. traf-fic
11. nap-kin
12. home-less
13. tall-est

Page 141
1. be-gin
2. so-fa
3. pi-lot
4. pil-lows
5. las-so
6. pup-pies
7. cried
8. ba-bies
9. la-dies
10. yel-low
11. spi-der
12. la-zy
13. co-zy
14. pa-per
15. mon-key
16. tur-key
17. ho-tel
18. pu-pils

Page 142
1. u-nit
2. dis-o-beyed
3. o-cean
4. a-live
5. Mex-i-co
6. o-pen
7. u-ni-form
8. dec-i-mals
9. pop-u-la-tion
10. par-a-graph
11. a-go
12. a-gain
13. a-muse
14. el-e-phant
15. a-ble
16. hab-i-ta-tion
17. grad-u-ate
18. a-pron
Stories will vary.
Check to see if words
from the list were
included.

Page 143
1. bo-a
2. du-et
3. po-et
4. po-li-o
5. du-el
6. ro-de-o
7. ra-di-o
8. di-et
9. i-de-a
10. ru-ined
11. i-de-as
12. gi-ants
13. cre-at-ing
14. li-on-ess
15. di-et-ing
16. pi-o-neers
17. fu-el
18. fo-li-o
Sentences will vary.
Check to see if some
of the words from the
above list are
included.

Page 144
1. bubble, bub-ble
2. simple, sim-ple
3. apple, ap-ple
4. ankle, an-kle
5. middle, mid-dle
6. turtle, tur-tle
7. purple, pur-ple
8. angle, an-gle
9. pickle, pic-kle
10. uncle, un-cle
11. little, lit-tle
12. table, ta-ble
13. muscle, mus-cle
14. able, a-ble
15. castle, cas-tle
16. needle, nee-dle

Page 145
Words with a single
consonant between
two vowels: lemon,
dragon, tiny, model,
visit, palace, finish,
wagon, robin, paper,
tiger, music
Words with two
vowels together
sounding separately:
poem, fluid, create,
giant, dial
Words with prefixes
or suffixes: powerful,
spoonful, smallest,
colder, rewriting,
flying, unkindly
Words with a single
vowel as a syllable:

document, usual,
polio, pioneer,
eternal, electric, odor,
idea, graduate,
pyramid

Page 146
1. re-, retie
2. un-, unhappy
3. dis-, dishonest
4. mis-, misplace
5. re-, repaint
6. -less, sleepless
7. ra-di-o
8. nim-ble
9. flu-id
10. pyr-a-mid
11. ti-ny
12. lem-on
13. hun-gry
14. dog-house
15. re-new

Page 147
1. powerful
2. whiteness,
   blinding
3. hoping
4. useful
5. unwise
6. disliked, stayed
7. displeased
8. dampness
9. playing,
   harmless
10. rebuilt
11. Suggestions:
    repaint,
    painting, painted
12. Suggestions:
    disagree,
    agreeable,
    agreement
13. Suggestions:
    owner, owned,
    pre-own
14. Suggestions:
    careful,
    carefully, cared
15. Suggestions:
    quickly, quicken
16. Suggestions:
    friendless, friendly,
    befriend

Page 149
1. i   6. a   11. n
2. e   7. j   12. k
3. h   8. f   13. g
4. m   9. d   14. o
5. l   10. b   15. c

Page 150
1. buddies, friends
2. baby, infant
3. quietly, silently
4. shop, store
5. present, gift
6. handsome,
   attractive
7. beautiful, pretty

Page 151
1. down   8. receive
2. short   9. left
3. dirty   10. no
4. outside   11. start
5. sell   12. wrong
6. lose   13. sink
7. day   14. boy

Page 152
1. hot, cold
2. read, write
3. mother, father
4. listen, speak
5. play, work
6. lost, found
7. noisy, quiet

Page 153
1. tie   7. bee
2. blew   8. wrap
3. pail   9. bear
4. one   10. eye
5. meat   11. sail
6. mail   12. eight

Page 154
1. four, for
2. see, sea
3. build, billed
4. sew, so
5. buy, by
6. right, Write
7. tale, tail

Page 155
lift—raise
find—locate
happy—glad
forest—woods
beautiful—pretty
large—big
purchase—buy
right—correct
asleep—awake
fat—thin
come—go
nothing—something
high—low
light—heavy
follow—lead
city—country
beat—beet
fair—fare
made—maid
break—brake
oar—or
steak—stake
wait—weight
week—weak

Page 156
1. ship, boat
2. gift, present
3. sack, bag
4. infant, baby
5. store, shop
6. up, down
7. healthy, sick
8. bloom, die
9. sun, moon
10. write, read
11. stairs
12. deer
13. ring
14. nose
15. knot

Page 157
Words should be in
the following order:
apple   muffin
bubbles   noodles
cookie   panda
dinosaur   spider
eagle   uncle
fish   violin
guitar   water
horse   zipper

Page 158
Set 1: paint, peanut,
   pickle, plant,
   pooch, proud, purse
Set 2: catch, center,
   church, city, class,
   coddle, cup
Set 3: sparkle, speed,
   splash, spout,
   spring, spunky
Set 4: thank, then,
   think, thought,
   thread, thumb

Page 159
1. cent, cattle, city,
   class
2. eagle, duck, dome

3. blade, bleed, blip
4. jacks, hug,
   hopeless
5. lock, little, letter
6. play, pot, pitch
7. milk, meddle,
   mock
8. steel, stick, stay
9. frock, freckle,
   fresh

Page 160
1. band, sheep, velvet
2. bus, ribbon, twin
3. nanny, dice, nickel
4. doze, wren, chip

Page 161
king: 175
locksmith: 181
library: 179
loan: 181
lifeguard: 179
list: 181
kangaroo: 175
kettle: 175
lawyer: 179
kind: 175
lemon: 179
live: 181
knife: 179
kennel: 175
loose: 181
trade: 251
supper: 248
trunk: 251
table: 248
scone: 245
sand: 245
tuba: 251
settle: 245
torch: 251
summer: 248
swamp: 248
shell: 245
ticket: 248
sift: 245
touch: 251

Page 162
baby • bug: balloon,
belt, boat, brick,
bubble
fan • fuzzy: fish,
float, foggy, frog,
funny
maid • mud:
marbles, maybe,
might, money,
monkey
name • nurse: night,
none, noodle, nudge,
number

Page 163
Beginning (A–I):
glow, creep, handle,
family, chimp, desert,
apple, bowl, eagle,
igloo
Middle (J–Q): mood,
lawn, laundry, jump,
purple, morning,
koala, quarter,
octagon, neigh
End (R–Z): wound,
snow, yawn, silly,
zipper, unicorn,
tickle, vowel, riddle,
riot

Page 164
1. Beginning
2. End
3. Middle
4. End
5. Beginning
6. Beginning
7. Middle

8. End
9. Middle
10. Beginning
11. End
12. Middle

Page 165
1. before   8. after
2. on   9. after
3. after   10. after
4. on   11. before
5. on   12. after
6. before   13. on
7. on   14. before

Page 166
1. 2   5. 3
2. 3   6. 2
3. 1   7. 1
4. 1   8. 2

Page 167
1. 1   5. 2
2. 2   6. 2
3. 2   7. 1
4. 1

Page 168
Synonyms
right—correct
weak—feeble
sent—dispatched
buy—purchase
Antonyms
right—wrong
weak—strong
sent—received
buy—sell
Homonyms
right—write
weak—week
sent—cent
buy—by

Page 169
leave—2, shore—1,
dab—3, rare—2,
grab—1, minute—1,
hoot—2

Page 170
1. synonym
2. antonym
3. homonym
4. homonym
5. synonym
6. homonym
7. antonym
8. homonym
9. synonym
10. antonym
11. blew
12. bear
13. mail
14. pail
15. blue
16. pale

Page 171
1. basket
2. batter
3. black
4. blue
5. bonnet
6. brick
7. brown
8. butter
9. deaf – deer
10. flick – flirt
11. ghost – gift
12. lantern – lap
13. mine – minnow
14. perk – persist
15. rasp – rating
16. sad – sail